MW00513789

# Windows

*Quick & Easy*

# A Visual Approach for the Beginner

Welcome to **Quick & Easy.** Designed for the true novice, this new series covers basic tasks in a simple, learn-by-doing fashion. If that sounds like old news to you, take a closer look.

**Quick & Easy** books are a bit like picture books. They're for people who would rather see and do than read and ponder. The books are colorful. They're full of illustrations, and accompanying text that is straightforward, concise, and easy to read.

But don't waste your time reading about our **Quick & Easy** books; start learning your new software package instead. This **Quick & Easy** book is just the place to start.

# Windows™
## Quick & Easy

## Robert Cowart

**SYBEX®**

San Francisco • Paris • Düsseldorf • Soest

Co-Author: Beverly Hill
Acquisitions Editor: Dianne King
Developmental Editor: Christian T.S. Crumlish
Editor: Brenda Kienan
Technical Editor: Sheila Dienes
Assistant Editor: Michelle Nance
Word Processor: Ann Dunn
Series Designers: Helen Bruno and Ingrid Owen
Production Artist: Suzanne Albertson
Graphic Illustrator: John Corrigan
Page Layout and Typesetting: Dina F Quan, Deborah Maizels, and Alissa Feinberg
Proofreader/Production Assistant: Elisabeth Dahl
Indexer: Nancy Guenther
Cover Designer: Archer Design
Cover Illustrator: Richard Miller

Screen reproductions produced with Collage Plus.
Collage Plus is a trademark of Inner Media Inc.

SYBEX is a registered trademark of SYBEX Inc.

TRADEMARKS: SYBEX has attempted throughout this book to distinguish proprietary trademarks from descriptive terms by following the capitalization style used by the manufacturer.

SYBEX is not affiliated with any manufacturer.

Every effort has been made to supply complete and accurate information. However, SYBEX assumes no responsibility for its use, nor for any infringement of the intellectual property rights of third parties which would result from such use.

Copyright ©1993 SYBEX Inc., 2021 Challenger Drive, Alameda, CA 94501. World rights reserved. No part of this publication may be stored in a retrieval system, transmitted, or reproduced in any way, including but not limited to photocopy, photograph, magnetic or other record, without the prior agreement and written permission of the publisher.

Library of Congress Card Number: 92-62086
ISBN: 0-89588-769-X

Manufactured in the United States of America
10 9 8 7 6 5 4 3 2

To my brother Jack for his humorous influence.

# ACKNOWLEDGMENTS

●

I want to thank those who helped make this book possible. First, thanks to editor-in-chief Dr. Rudolph Langer and acquisitions editor Dianne King for their continued support in my writing for SYBEX.

Next, I want to thank the people in the editorial and production departments for their various toils. Though a small book, Windows Quick & Easy required exceptional care in both those departments due to its brief editorial style and four-color printing. Particular thanks go to developmental editor Christian Crumlish and editor Brenda Kienan. Thanks also to technical editor Sheila Dienes; assistant editor Michelle Nance; typesetters Deborah Maizels, Alissa Feinberg, and Dina Quan; illustrator John Corrigan; production artist Suzanne Albertson; proofreader Elisabeth Dahl; and indexer Nancy Guenther.

On another side of the fence, many many thanks to my co-writer, Beverly Hill for her writing, editorial overview, and superb crisis management. I certainly appreciated that she sacrificed weekends and late nights, and that she continually ran interference for me.

Last and certainly not least, many heartfelt thanks to the SYBEX sales and marketing department—the people who sell and promote these books, making them available worldwide. These folks are on the road an incredible amount of time, and have a very difficult job.

Thanks once again to you all!

# Contents
## at a Glance
•

# Contents

Computers are supposed to make life easier. But let's face it—ten years ago, all you needed to write a letter was a typewriter and a bottle of white-out. Nowadays it seems you need a degree in computer science and a training class in WordPerfect.

But things are getting better. You may have heard that Windows takes much of the guesswork and pain out of using your PC. This is definitely true. Still, you have to learn Windows, and even as a veteran computer user, I was confused a bit at first.

## What Makes It Quick & Easy?

As you probably know, a ton of information about Windows is available. Everyone from book publishers to seminar promoters is rushing to cash in on the Windows phenomenon. With new Windows titles appearing daily on bookstore shelves, it's no surprise that buyers are confused about which one to purchase. Some of these books are quite hefty tomes. (For example, I've written another book about Windows, *Mastering Windows 3.1 Special Edition*, which is about 1000 pages long!)

Not everybody wants to know *everything* about Windows. Some people want just enough information to get around. A huge book would end up sitting on those people's shelves—just another reason not to learn to use their computer! If all you want to do is write letters or set up simple spreadsheets, this book is for you.

*Windows Quick & Easy* is one of a series of new books written and designed for newcomers to computers. With Quick & Easy books, you don't have to be a computer jock, or even comfortable with computers, to follow the instructions. In short order you'll become proficient with the product that the book covers.

In *Windows Quick & Easy* I'll lead you through all the basics of Windows in about 250 pages. You'll be up and running with Windows in no time. I've written it based on my experience with people who are either afraid of computers, or completely inexperienced, so I've been particularly careful to leave out the computer gobble-de-gook that could bog you down.

I've written most of the book in step-by-step instructions accompanied by clear four-color pictures to make following along even easier. The pictures show exactly what you should expect to see on the screen and the text tells you exactly what you're supposed to do. Flip through the book for a minute and notice also that many of the pictures have labels on them, identifying portions of the screen, or supplying additional information about a procedure. You can actually learn almost all you need to know just by looking at the pictures.

I've made every effort to tell you only what you'll need to know to learn and use Windows quickly—sparing you the boring or nonessential. Where some addition information would be useful to you, I've often put it in an aside, called a note, printed in a different color.

The book is broken down into 24 bite-sized lessons. At the beginning of each lesson is an estimated time so you'll have an idea how long each one will take.

## What's Wrong with the Manual?

Yes, Microsoft Windows comes with a manual, as do other software products. But out of necessity manuals tell you everything about a product, and they are organized as reference books rather than learning aids. Often they're written in techno-babble instead of plain English.

By the time you're done reading this book, you'll really be up and running with Windows. You'll know how to get around the screens, run typical programs, run DOS from within Windows, work with dialog boxes, use the File Manager to keep your files organized, and use the major Windows Accessory programs—Notepad, Cardfile, Calendar, Write, and Paint.

## Before We Get Going

Just a few notes before you start—first off, the lessons and steps in this book are designed to teach you Windows in an order that makes sense. Though you may be tempted to skip around between lessons, my advice is to do them in order. That way, new terms or concepts that I build on will make sense, and you'll have the reassurance of having your screen match what you see in the pictures on the page.

Secondly, there are bound to be some slight differences between what you see on your screen and what's shown in the book, because of the differences between types of computers, or because someone may have used your computer and adjusted Windows a bit already. I've tried to write the examples and instructions to prevent this from happening. If your screen looks seriously different from the illustrations in the book, have someone who knows about Windows try to get you back to "square one."

With that said, you can kick back, move on to Lesson 1 and start learning how Windows can make your PC much easier to use.

# Windows Basics

**T**his book is divided into four parts. In Part One, I'll introduce you to Windows and quickly show you the "lay of the land." You'll learn about the elements of the Windows screen, and how to interact with them using your mouse. I'll show you how to start up Windows, reposition and resize various windows, run a program, use menus and dialog boxes, and finally, how to quit Windows and take a break. If this sounds like a lot, don't worry. You'll be done in no time.

# Starting Windows

# 1

**W**indows is a type of computer program called a *graphical user interface*, or GUI (pronounced "gooey"), which makes using your computer easier. With Windows, instead of getting things done by typing in cryptic keyboard commands, you just "point" the mouse and "click" at objects on your computer screen. You can learn new programs more easily and get your work done with less hassle.

Windows is called Windows because your work appears in little boxes that look like window panes on the screen. You can work on a letter and a spreadsheet, and play a game of solitaire all during one session, keeping each in separate windows. You can visually adjust the sizes and positions of the windows to your liking. You can also compare material in two windows, copy between them, and so forth. This makes working with your computer that much more efficient. Before Windows, you typically had to quit one DOS application program before running another. Why should a work tool force you to think about only one job at a time? In the real world, you shuffle tasks around on your desk, answer the phone, jot down a few notes, and then read yesterday's mail. Windows lets you set up your working environment in much the same way.

**● Note** For this book, we'll assume Windows is already installed on your computer. If it isn't, follow the instructions in the Windows manual or get a friend or dealer to help you.

## Getting Windows Going

Each time you turn on your computer, you'll let it "boot up" DOS, and give it a command to have Windows take over the show.

**1.** If your A: drive has a floppy disk in it, remove the disk.

**2.** Turn your computer and screen on. In a moment, your computer boots up, and the familiar DOS prompt appears. It usually looks something like **C:\>**.

**3.** Type **win** and press ↵.

**4.** The Windows sign-on screen appears, and (you may have to wait about 30 seconds or so) then Windows is loaded into your computer.

Quick & Easy

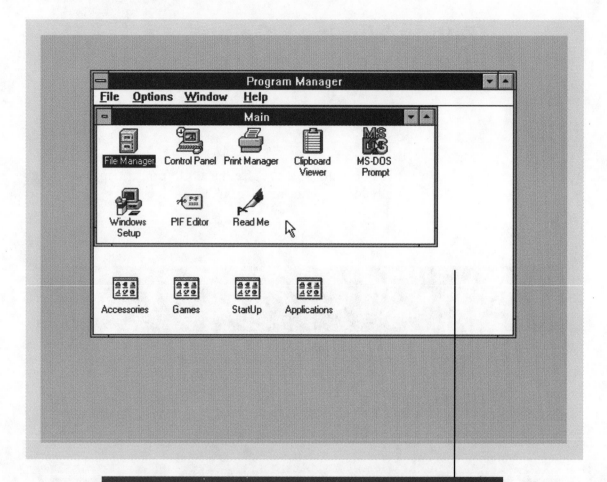

**The Program Manager screen you see when Windows starts.**

This illustration shows Windows as it appears the first time you run it.
The exact arrangement of items on your screen will vary depending on
how you left Windows last time. Don't worry if your screen looks a little
different this time. We'll take care of that later, as you learn how to adjust
the sizes of windows and rearrange the little pictures.

In the next lesson I'll show you around the Windows screen.

# 2

# Recognizing Parts of the Screen

If you're absolutely new to Windows, but have some experience using a PC, you're probably wondering, "What *is* all that weird stuff on my screen?" Where there used to be just a blank screen with a DOS prompt, or programs that only display text, now there are little pictures and boxes on the screen. At first this can be confusing or intimidating to new Windows users, but using Windows is pretty simple once you learn just a few of its elements. Since these same elements are used by all Windows programs, getting the basics down will pay off quickly. Windows makes PCs more "user friendly." Once you know your way around the screen, you can figure out a lot of things for yourself, because things are done pretty much the same way in every program.

Take a look at the picture below, and at your screen, and check out the major components as you compare the two. If someone has been working in Windows on your machine, your screen might be arranged a little differently than this one—notice the features themselves, whatever their arrangement on your screen.

*Quick Easy*

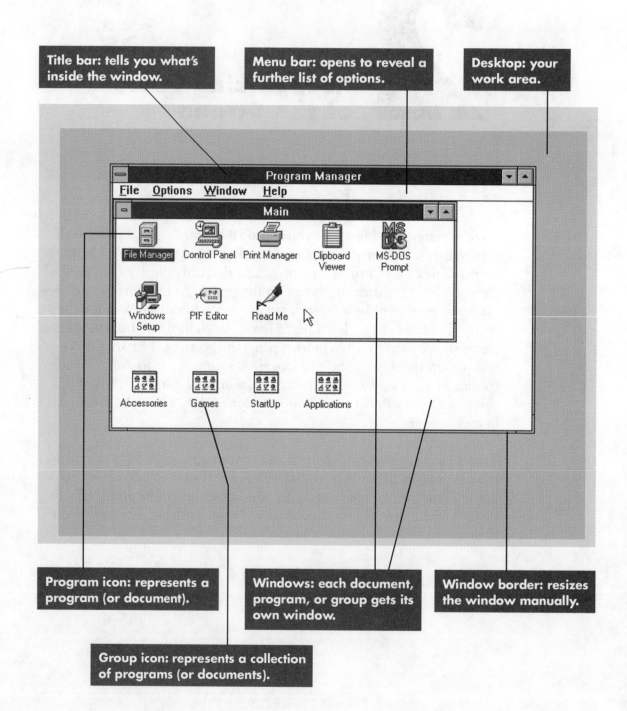

**Title bar: tells you what's inside the window.**

**Menu bar: opens to reveal a further list of options.**

**Desktop: your work area.**

Program Manager

File   Options   Window   Help

Main

File Manager   Control Panel   Print Manager   Clipboard Viewer   MS-DOS Prompt

Windows Setup   PIF Editor   Read Me

Accessories   Games   StartUp   Applications

**Program icon: represents a program (or document).**

**Windows: each document, program, or group gets its own window.**

**Window border: resizes the window manually.**

**Group icon: represents a collection of programs (or documents).**

## Desktop

The *desktop* is your overall work area in Windows—essentially the whole screen. It's called the desktop because Windows uses it in a way that's similar to the way you'd use the surface of a desk. When you start a day's work, you probably decide what projects you're going to undertake. You pull out a report, check your calendar, and grab a calculator, or whatever. You organize everything at your desk and then dig into your work. But you don't just start writing on the top of your desk, right? You have to have a piece of paper to write on. With Windows it's much the same, except that you retrieve material, and arrange and perform tasks using graphical representations of your work projects and tools. You put each task, document, tool, or game in a window on your computer's "desktop." You can have virtually as many windows on your desktop as you like, and you can jump between them easily.

## Window Borders

*Window borders* define a window's edges. You can also use the borders to resize a window (more on this later).

## Title Bar

The name of each program or document appears at the top of its window, in the *title bar*. In the picture above, the two title bars read *Program Manager* and *Main*. If you're running another application, such as WordPerfect, you'll see its name in the title bar. The title bar also indicates which window is *active*. Though you can have lots of windows on the screen, only one—the one you're working in—is active at any given time. When you activate a window, it jumps in front of other windows that might be obscuring it, and its title bar changes color or intensity.

## Menu Bar

The *menu bar* appears just below the title bar of a window, and contains a number of words, such as File, Edit, or Help. These are the names of *menus* that open to reveal commands you use to perform tasks. The number of menu names varies from application to application, but the menus work more or less the same way in all Windows programs.

## Program and Group Icons

Each *program icon* represents a program or document. A collection, or group of programs or documents, might be represented by a *group icon*.

## Moving Right Along

With a little Windows geography under your belt, now you can move ahead to the next lesson. There you'll begin experimenting with these parts of the Windows screen.

# 3 Moving the Mouse, Clicking, and Dragging

Y ou can survive in Windows without a mouse, but most Windows users have one, and this book assumes you'll be mousing around. As you gain more experience with Windows, I'll explain how to use the keyboard, but mouse procedures will predominate.

If you don't know how to use your mouse, read through this lesson for some hands-on experience.

## Finding the Mouse and Its Pointer

The mouse, a little contraption that you push around on your desk, has a cord that looks like a tail sticking out the back—thus, its name. Mice come in all manner of shapes and sizes. Some have no tail at all but run by remote. Some have to be operated on a special metallic-looking pad that has a grid pattern on it. Others, called *track balls*, sit stationary and have a ball on the top that you roll with your hand. (Standard mice have a ball on the bottom that rotates as you move the mouse across the desk.) Some laptops have a mini track ball built right into them or a mouse attached to the side of the computer. Whatever their design, all mice have two or three buttons on them, and all mice perform the same functions.

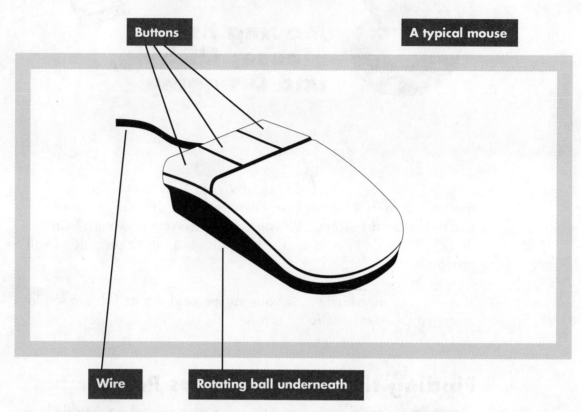

**Buttons**

**A typical mouse**

**Wire**

**Rotating ball underneath**

When you slide the mouse across your desk (or rotate the ball on top), something happens on the screen—an arrow, or cursor, moves around in relation to your hand's movements. This arrow is called the *mouse pointer.*

**1.** Locate your mouse. If you have a mouse pad, put the mouse down on that, not just anywhere on the desk.

**2.** Try moving the mouse around on your desk a bit now. Pull it toward you. Move it away from you. Notice that as you do this, the mouse pointer moves down and up on the screen. Move the mouse left and right. Same thing, right?

It takes a little hand-eye coordination, but soon you'll get the feel for how much hand movement is required to move the pointer a given distance on the screen.

> **● Note** If you're left-handed, you can change your mouse settings from the Control Panel, and reverse the mouse buttons so you can push the main button with your left index finger. See your Windows manual for details.

Moving the mouse pointer around on your screen is the first step in learning how to use the mouse. Once you have positioned the mouse pointer where you want it, you have to tell the computer what you want to do. To give the go-ahead signal, you push one of the buttons on the mouse. Usually it's the left one, which means that if you're moving the mouse with your right hand, you'll be pushing the button with your index finger. This process is called *point and click*.

## Clicking and Double-Clicking

There are two variations of button pushing. With the first, just called *clicking*, you simply push the button down briefly and release it. In the second, called *double-clicking*, you push the button down twice in quick succession and then let go. Try these steps to learn how to click:

**1.** Position the pointer on one of the icons on your screen.

**2.** Click the left mouse button once (only once!). If you click on a program icon, its title becomes highlighted. If you click on a group icon, a little box pops up above it. (This is called a *menu*. We'll talk about menus later.)

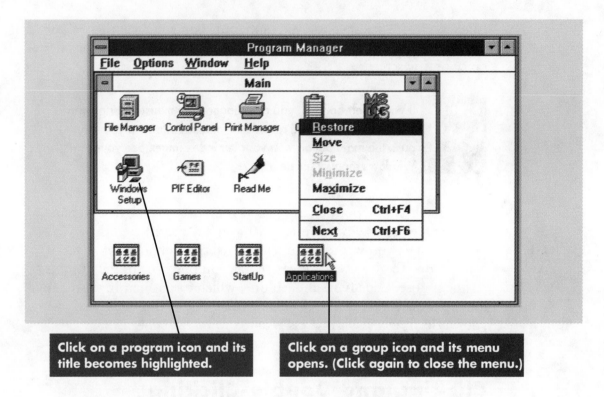

**Click on a program icon and its title becomes highlighted.**

**Click on a group icon and its menu opens. (Click again to close the menu.)**

**3.** If, in step 2, you clicked on a group icon and the little box appeared above it, click once again on the icon. The box disappears. If you clicked on a program icon, it was only highlighted, so there is nothing to be undone.

Double-clicking is a slight variation on clicking. You still position the pointer on an object (like an icon), just as with single-clicking. But then you click twice in fast succession. Double-clicking is often used for running or quitting a program. The trick with double-clicking is to get your timing down. If your clicks aren't close enough together, nothing happens.

Try double-clicking:

**1.** Position the pointer on the **Program Manager** control box.

**2.** Now double-click on the control box. (If you didn't click fast enough, the control menu appeared. Click once again to close it, and try again.) You'll know if you did it right because your screen will look like this illustration.

**Double-click on the Program Manager's Control box and see what happens.**

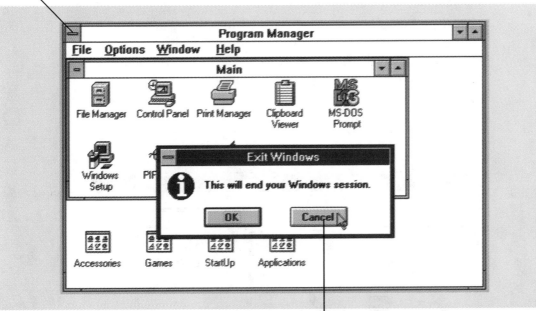

**Click on the word *Cancel* and you return to Windows.**

**3.** Click on the word **Cancel**. You don't want to quit Windows just yet.

## Dragging

To *drag* with the mouse, you position the pointer on an item, hold down the button, and move the mouse in the direction that you want

to drag the item on the screen. When you reach the desired destination, release the mouse button. Dragging is used to move graphics or icons around on your screen.

Practice some dragging by doing the following:

**1.** Move the mouse pointer to the bottom of the **Program Manager** window, where you should see four little icons.

**2.** Position the pointer over the **Applications** icon (or any other one, for that matter—it doesn't matter which). Press and hold down the button while you move the mouse to the right. The arrow adopts the shape of the icon (the icon's name temporarily disappears) and as you move the mouse pointer, the icon follows your movements.

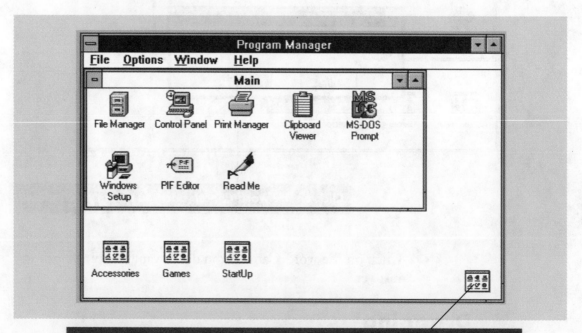

Drag the Applications group icon to a new location and notice that the pointer changes to look like the icon. Release it and see what happens.

**3.** Release the mouse button. The icon is left at the new position (and its name reappears).

**4.** Now practice your skill a bit more by dragging the icon back to approximately its former position.

You'll do a lot of dragging while working in Windows. In later lessons, you'll learn more about moving windows, icons, and files by dragging.

Good. You're now up to speed on basic mouse procedures. You can go ahead to the next lesson where you'll learn more about windows.

# Arranging Your Windows

**4**

You'll probably want to work with more than one project at a time. Once you have a bunch of windows open, though, they start to overlap and obscure each other. To eliminate the clutter and set things up on the desktop the way you like, a few tricks will serve you well.

## Pushing a Window Around

Often you'll simply want to reposition a window to another area of the screen. This is done using the dragging techniques you learned in the last lesson when you moved the group icon. We'll do a little more this time.

**1.** Position the pointer over the **Program Manager** window's title bar (the one that reads *Program Manager*) and press and hold the mouse button.

**2.** Move the mouse around in a big circle. Notice that the outline of the window moves to follow the motion of your hand. The outline will even "fall off" the edge of the screen if you go too far. That's OK. Just notice that you can move it pretty much wherever you want it.

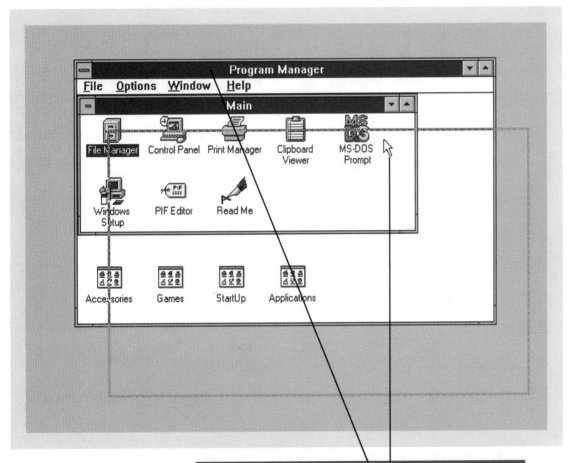

Drag the Program Manager title bar and the outline
of the window moves with the mouse pointer.

**3.** When the bottom of the outline is close to the bottom of
your screen, release the button to drop the window into its
new location.

*Quick Easy*

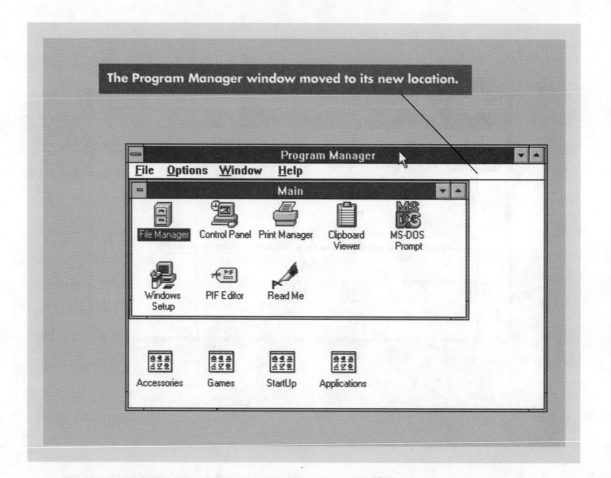

The Program Manager window moved to its new location.

You might have noticed that inside the Program Manager window there's a smaller window called *Main*. Though it's part of the Program Manager window, this is also a window in its own right. Play with that one for a moment.

**1.** Try dragging the smaller **Main** window around within the larger **Program Manager** window just to see what happens.

**2.** Drop it in a few different places. Notice that you can't move it beyond the border of the Program Manager window. This is because it's part of Program Manager and is what's called a *child* window. (The larger Program Manager window is called the *parent* window.) Keep this in mind. It'll come up later when we run programs.

**Some windows have smaller windows within them. The larger (outer) one is called the *parent* window.**

**The smaller (inner) window is called the *child* window.**

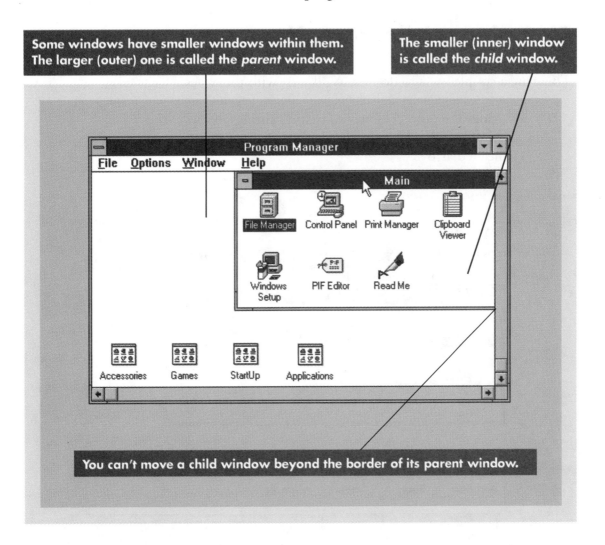

**You can't move a child window beyond the border of its parent window.**

**● Note** Even if you've moved a window so far off the screen that you think you've lost it, the window isn't gone. You can always get it back, and nothing will be lost. Just point at the little bit of title bar that's showing, and drag the window back into view.

**3.** Now move the window to where you want to leave it and release the mouse button.

## Changing a Window's Size

So much for repositioning a window. How about changing its size? There are a couple ways to do this. We'll start with the easiest.

**1.** Move the pointer slowly so that it's sitting on top of the Main window's border. Its shape will change to a double-headed arrow.

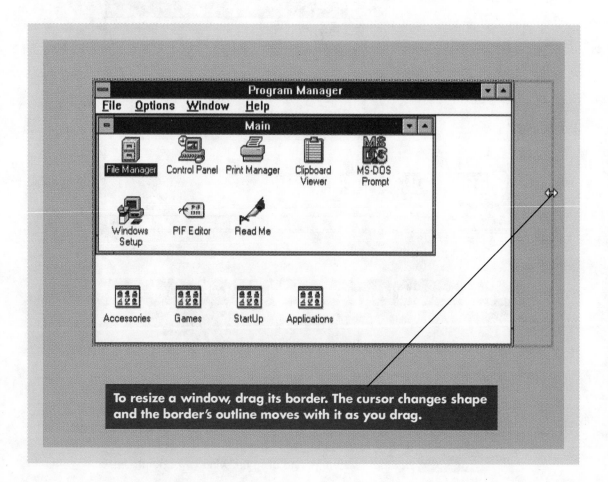

To resize a window, drag its border. The cursor changes shape and the border's outline moves with it as you drag.

**2.** While the pointer is in its new shape, press the mouse button and then drag the border. Just a portion of the window's outline will move with the pointer.

**3.** Release the button, and the window resizes.

If resizing didn't work, try again, aiming more carefully before you press the mouse button. The pointer has to have the double-headed arrow shape for resizing to work.

**● Note** The icons may rearrange themselves to accommodate the window's new size.

You can drag any part of a window's border—the top, bottom, sides, or even the corners. Dragging the corner lets you resize the window both horizontally and vertically at once. Experiment with moving the border sides and corners until you feel comfortable with the technique.

## Maximizing a Window

You might want to see as much of, say, a newsletter or spreadsheet as possible and eliminate the unnecessary visual distraction of seeing other windows. You could do this manually—by dragging the border and repositioning, as you just learned. But there's an easier way—with the window's *Maximize* button. It makes the window grow as large as the full screen.

**1.** Click on the Program Manager's **Maximize** button.

*Quick&Easy*

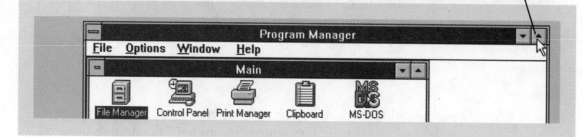

Click the Maximize button to make a window as big as possible.

**2.** Notice that the Program Manager's outer border has disappeared. Look at the upper-right corner, where the Maximize button used to be. It has changed to a *Restore* button.

**3.** Click on the **Restore** button, and the window will return to its previous size.

## Maximizing a Child Window

Now for something a little trickier. You just maximized a parent window. What happens when you maximize a child window? How big can it get?

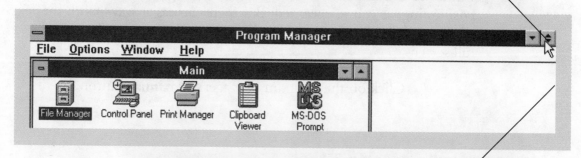

The Maximize button changes to a Restore button when the window is maxed out. Click on it and the window returns to its previous size.

When a window is maximized, its outer border disappears.

**1.** Click on the Main window's **Maximize** button.

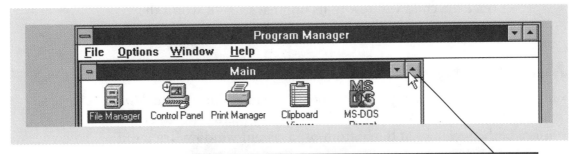

**Child windows have Maximize buttons, too. Click here to maximize the *Main* window within its parent window.**

The Main window will grow, but it's restricted to the size of the Program Manager window. Just as a parent window can be no larger than the screen containing it, a child window can be only as big as its parent window.

**When you maximize a child window, the parent's title bar shows both windows' names. Here the word *Main* is tacked onto *Program Manager*.**

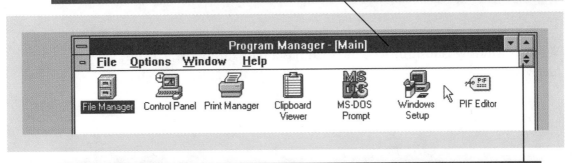

**A new Restore button shows up on the menu bar. This is the child window's Restore button. If you click this, the Main window returns to its previous size.**

**2.** Notice that there's now a **Restore** button in the menu bar. This is a little confusing since it's right below the place where the Restore button was last time. Click on it and re-duce the child window to its original size—it works the same way as any Restore button. Try this now.

## Minimizing a Window

One last thing about sizing windows before we take a break: the *Mini-mize* button turns any window into an itty-bitty picture (icon) at the bottom of the screen or at the bottom of its parent window. Try it out:

**1.** Click on the Program Manager's **Minimize** button.

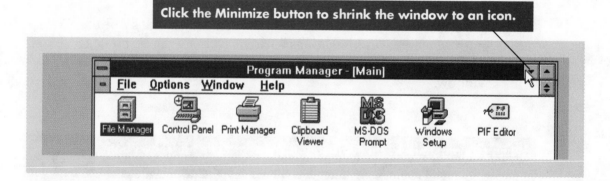

**Click the Minimize button to shrink the window to an icon.**

When a window is minimized, the icon has a name under it, so you know what it is.

**The Program Manager window minimized to an icon.**

**2.** To restore the icon to a window, double-click it. Voilà! The window comes back up on the screen.

Now you know what windows are and how to mess with them: how to reposition them, resize them, temporarily minimize them to an icon, and then restore them. And you know about most of the little buttons and on the screen. A few more lessons and you'll have all the basics under your belt so you can actually do something useful with Windows.

Turn to the next short lesson where you'll see how to quit Windows and take a break.

# 5

## Exiting Windows

If you need to take a break to escape your computer anxiety, deal with the kids, or attend a meeting, you'll want to know how to quit Windows gracefully. Use this procedure any time you want to power down.

Your computer is not like a TV or a blender. You can't pull the plug or hit the switch and turn the dang thing off at the drop of a hat. First you have to tell it that you're finished, so that Windows can do a little housekeeping to save any work in progress.

Even if you are running a program in Windows and you quit that program, you'll want to exit Windows and get back to the DOS prompt *before* turning off your computer.

Here's how:

1. Aim the pointer at the **Program Manager** control box.

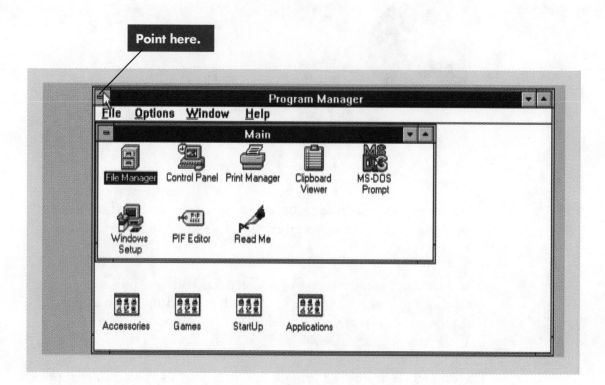

Point here.

2. Double-click. A *dialog box* pops up in the middle of the screen (you'll get well acquainted with dialog boxes in later lessons) informing you that you're about to end your Windows session.

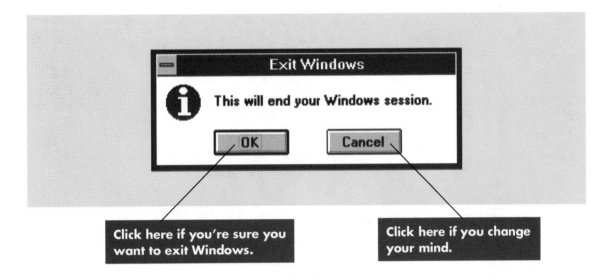

**Click here if you're sure you want to exit Windows.**

**Click here if you change your mind.**

**3.** Click on **OK** if you really want out. If you change your mind or you didn't mean to exit Windows, click on **Cancel**.

**4.** You should see the familiar DOS prompt: **C:\>**.

**5.** Now you can turn off your computer and screen.

**● Note** You must save and close the documents you're working on before you exit Windows. Later in this book you'll learn how. This will add another step or two to the procedure above. Until then, keep in mind that you must save and close your documents first, then exit Windows.

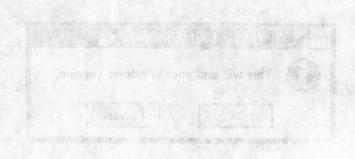

# Running Programs

I explained in the Introduction that Windows makes running your programs easier. Here in Part Two I'll talk about running programs—and how to create, save, and print your documents. You'll learn the essential techniques for using typical Windows programs such as Word for Windows or Write. You'll also learn a bit about how to run your DOS programs within Windows, since you may not be ready to replace your old tried-and-true DOS software with Windows versions quite yet.

15 MINUTES

# Running Applications

If you quit Windows after the last lesson, start it up again. Go back to Lesson 1 if you don't remember how.

Most Windows programs have some common features, which make them easy to learn. The way you interact with, say, WordPerfect for Windows is similar to the way you interact with Lotus 1-2-3 for Windows, even though one is a word processor and the other is a spreadsheet.

You know how to move windows around the screen. Next you need to learn how to start a program, use its menus, choose commands, and re-spond to dialog boxes.

## Firing Up a Program

There are a number of ways to run a program from Windows. The easiest is from the Program Manager, so that's where we'll start. As examples, we'll use a couple of the freebie programs that come with Windows.

The Program Manager window should be on your screen. Unless you've been experimenting on your own, you've only seen the Main window thus far, with its eight little icons. As you may remember from Lesson 2, each one of the icons (File Manager, Control Panel, etc.) represents a program that can be run by double-clicking on the icon. Remember, too, that the icons below the Main window (Accessories, Games, etc.) are *group* icons representing collections of programs that have something in common.

**1.** First, let's play with the Calculator, which is like a hand-held calculator that's on your screen instead of in your hand. Since the Calculator is stored in the Accessories group, you first have to double-click on the icon labeled **Accessories**.

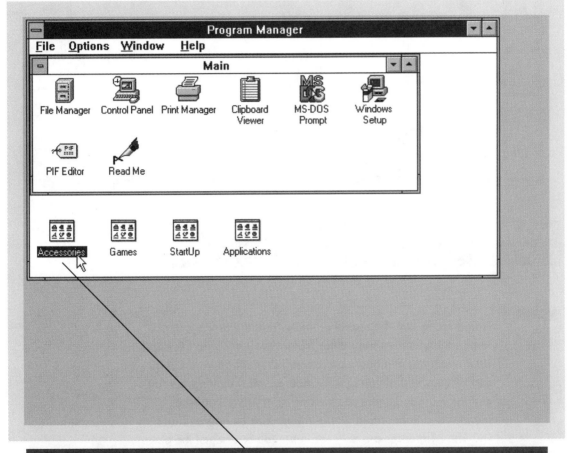

**Double-click on the Accessories group icon to see the programs that are stored in it.**

The Accessories group opens in its own child window, displaying all the free programs you got with Windows.

*Quick Easy*

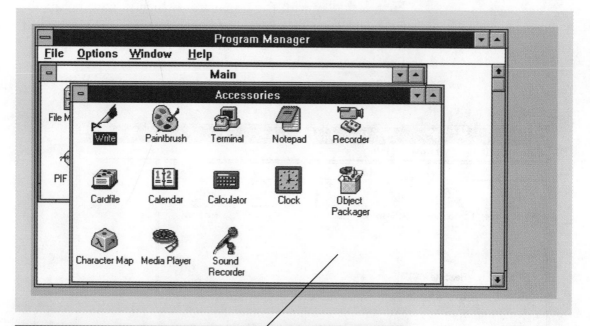

**The Accessories group window appears. This is a second child window within the Program Manager parent window.**

● **Note**  From here on out, the size of windows and the arrangement of icons on your screen may differ from what you see in this book. This is because Windows remembers any changes in sizing and placement that you make. Once you start moving windows and icons around, these changes will carry over between sessions and your screen won't always look like mine. That's OK. The differences are only cosmetic. You can adjust the place-ment and size of a window, if you need to, by dragging it. I've moved the Program Manager window to the upper-left corner of the desktop and resized it to make room for the exercises we're going to do in this section.

**2.** Double-click on the **Calculator** (adjust the window first if you need to).

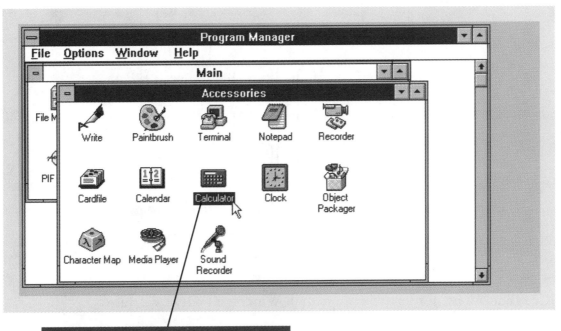

Double-click on the Calculator to run it.

The program now runs, and something akin to a hand-held calculator pops up on your screen.

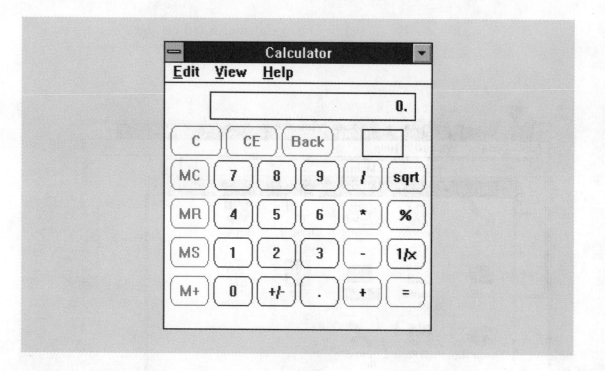

Congratulations. You've run a program in Windows. Pretty easy, wasn't it? Now to play with it a bit.

## Using Drop-Down Menus

Notice that the Calculator has a menu bar at the top, just like the Program Manager does. There are three words on it: Edit, View, and Help.

Each of these represents a drop-down menu that you can open. Here's an example:

**1.** Click once on the word **View**. The View menu opens and contains two choices:

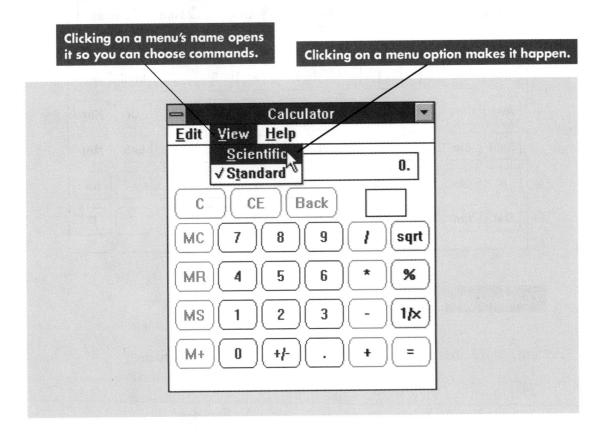

**Clicking on a menu's name opens it so you can choose commands.**

**Clicking on a menu option makes it happen.**

Notice the little check mark next to Standard. This means that "standard" mode is currently activated.

**2.** Click on **Scientific** to change the view.

Calculator goes scientific.

The command is executed and the Calculator changes to a new format.

**3.** Open the **View** menu again, and notice that Scientific now has the check mark next to it. Now choose **Standard**. The Calculator reverts to its previous configuration.

**• Note** If the Calculator suddenly disappeared from view, you may have clicked outside of its boundary. When you do this, the window you've clicked on will take over, and move in front of the Calculator. If you accidentally clicked on the Program Manager window, for example, that would happen. Press **Alt** and **Tab** together, and the Calculator will pop up again.

OK. Now you know how to choose commands from menus. While you have the Calculator open, exercise your mouse skills by doing a few calculations. You click on the numbers to enter them, just as if you were pressing the keys. You can also enter numbers from the keyboard. Press the Esc key to clear the display.

## Closing a Program with a Drop-Down Menu

Suppose you want to close the Calculator because you're through working with it. Here's how:

1. Click once on the **Calculator** control box.

**You open the Control menu by clicking once in the upper-left corner of its window.**

**Close any program by opening its Control menu and choosing Close.**

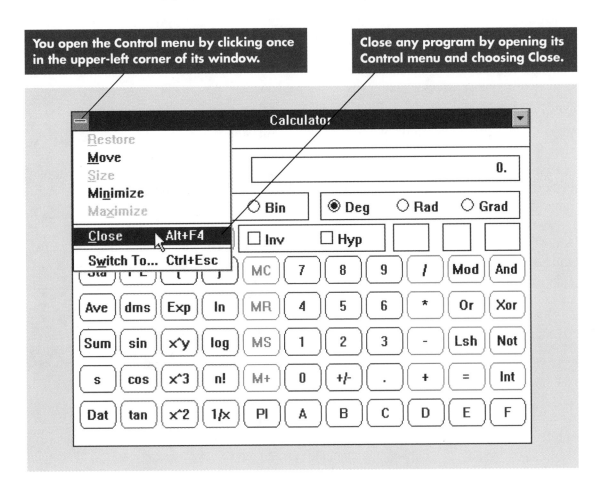

The Control menu opens. There are a bunch of commands here.

**2.** Choose **Close**. Calculator closes, and you're returned to the next available program. In this case, it's Program Manager.

 **Note** You can quit any Windows program using these basic steps. An even faster way to quit a program is to double-click on the program's Control box.

## Commands That Ask You Questions

The commands you just chose were simple ones. All you had to do was open the menu and click on the command. Some commands require a little more. They might ask you to choose from a list of options or type in some text.

When commands require additional information, a *dialog box* will pop up on your screen. Typically, you'll fill in the requested information, then click on OK to make it happen. You've seen one dialog box already — if you exited Windows at the end of Lesson 5, you had to click on OK to exit. That was a simple one. We'll experiment with a few others now.

After Calculator is closed, Program Manager should be showing on your screen. The Accessories window is probably open, but you may be able to still see the Main group, behind the Accessories window. Don't worry about the arrangement—it doesn't matter at this point.

**1.** Open the File menu by clicking on the word **File**.

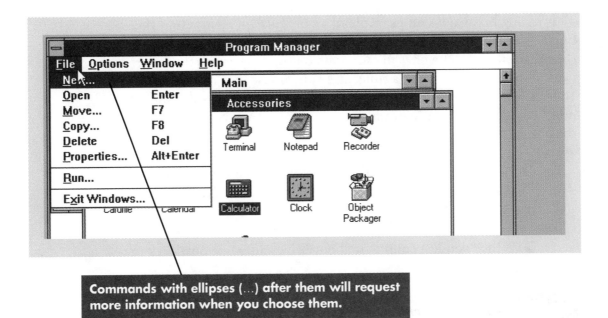

Commands with ellipses (...) after them will request more information when you choose them.

**2.** Notice that some commands end in three dots. If you choose any of these commands, you'll be asked to fill in some information before going on.

**3.** From the menu, choose **New** by clicking on it.

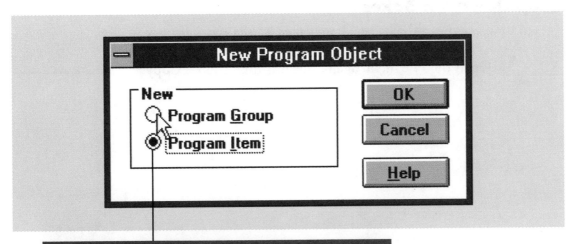

Radio buttons. Only one can be on at a time. Click on a button to activate it, and all the others will be inactive.

This dialog box shows an example of *radio buttons*. Remember the buttons on old car radios? When one is pushed down, it's *on* and the others are *off*. The ones in Windows dialog boxes work the same way. Only one can be on at a time, and you choose by clicking on it. You can tell which one is currently set "on" because it has a dot in the middle. Program Item is currently selected. (Don't worry about what the box is for. We're just using this as an example.)

**4.** Click on a button that's not active, and see the dot jump to it. It turns on and the other option turns off. Now, to set it back again, repeat.

**5.** Once you feel confident about using radio buttons, click on **Cancel**.

> **• Note** *Cancel* is your panic button while in Windows. Almost all dialog boxes have a Cancel button that you can click on to back out of whatever you've gotten yourself into. When you click Cancel, it's as if you never opened the dialog box, regardless of what changes or settings you made prior to canceling. (Often the Esc has the same effect as clicking on Cancel.)

## Drop-Down List Boxes

Here's another type of dialog box item called a *drop-down list box*.

**1.** Open the **File** menu again, but this time choose **Copy**.

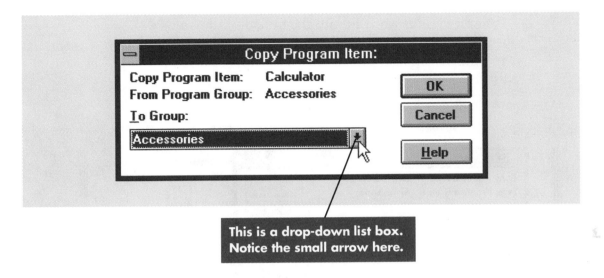

This is a drop-down list box.
Notice the small arrow here.

The resulting dialog box contains a drop-down list box. Drop-down list boxes contain a list of possible choices sort of like a menu.

**2.** Click on the little arrow on the right side of the box and the list opens up.

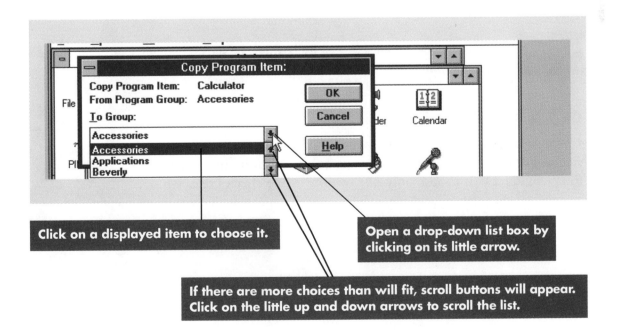

Click on a displayed item to choose it.

Open a drop-down list box by clicking on its little arrow.

If there are more choices than will fit, scroll buttons will appear. Click on the little up and down arrows to scroll the list.

**3.** If all the choices won't fit into the little drop-down box,
*scroll buttons* may appear. Click on the lower scroll button
and the list scrolls down. Click on the upper button and the
list scrolls up.

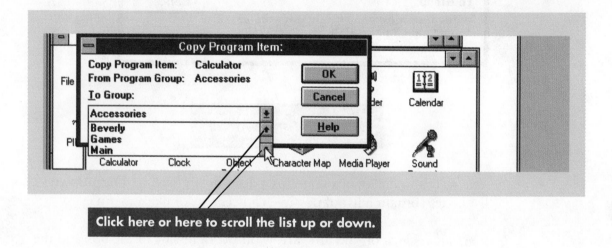

Click here or here to scroll the list up or down.

**4.** Click on **Cancel** to close the dialog box.

● **Note**  The group names you have in your list box may be slightly
different from what you see in the picture above.

## Check Boxes

*Check boxes* allow you to choose several options at once. For example,
you might want some text to appear as bold *and* underlined. Radio buttons would let you choose only one option, while check boxes will let

you turn on one, or more. Here's an example from a Microsoft Word for Windows dialog box:

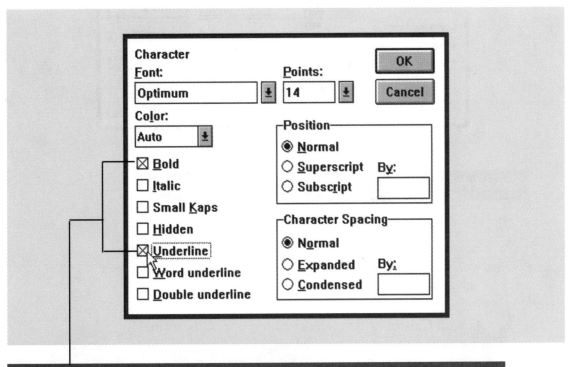

Some check boxes from a Word for Windows 1.1 dialog box. Note that several can be set on at a time. Here both Underline and Bold are turned on.

Let's experiment with a check box now.

**1.** On the **Program Manager** menu bar, click on **File**.

**2.** From the menu, click on **Properties**.

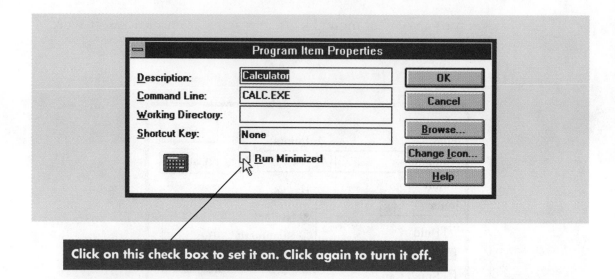

Click on this check box to set it on. Click again to turn it off.

**3.** Click on the check box for **Run Minimized**. Notice that a check mark (X) appears in the box. This indicates the option is selected. Click again and it goes off.

**4.** Click on **Cancel** to remove the dialog box without making any changes to the Program Manager.

## List Boxes

List boxes are similar to drop-down list boxes. Try this to see one:

**1.** Open the **Help** menu.

**2.** Click on **Search for Help on....**

**A typical list box.**

**Click on a list item to choose it.**

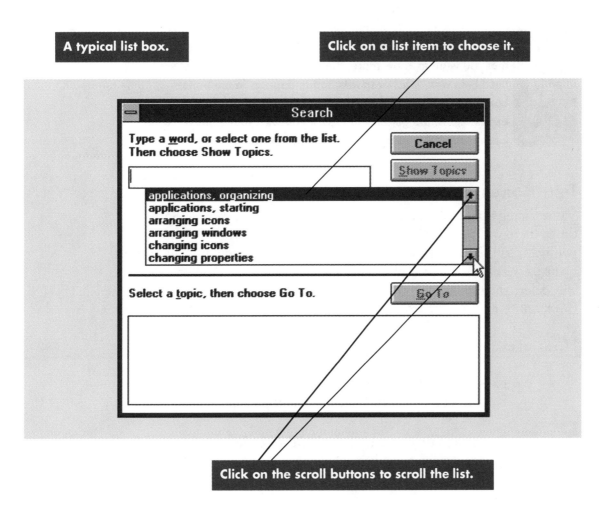

**Click on the scroll buttons to scroll the list.**

**3.** Click on the scroll buttons to scroll through the list of help items.

**4.** Return to Program Manager by clicking on the **Cancel** button.

**• Note** The top part of the Help dialog box lets you pick a general area that you want to know more about. Once you choose what you need help with, a list of specific topics appears in the bottom box. Choosing one of these displays a screenful or more of explanations and guidance to assist you with your task. You'll learn more about using the Help dialog box later.

## Text Boxes

Some dialog boxes ask you to type in text from the keyboard. Sometimes there will be text already typed in for you—a probable choice. If you want to keep it as is, leave it alone. Or you can type in what you want. If the existing text is already highlighted, the first key you press will delete the highlighted entry. If it isn't highlighted, you can use Backspace to erase the text, and then you can type in new text.

Here's an example:

**1.** Back at the Main window, click *once* on the **Clipboard Viewer** icon. It should become highlighted.

**2.** Open the **File** menu and choose **Properties**.
Notice the four text boxes.

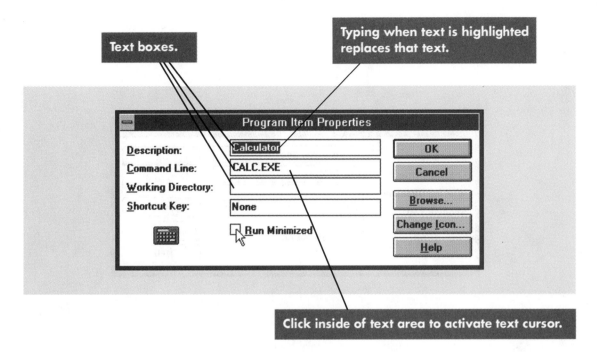

Text boxes.

Typing when text is highlighted replaces that text.

Click inside of text area to activate text cursor.

**3.** Notice in the **Description** text box that Clipboard Viewer is highlighted. Type the letter **T**. The T replaces all the text that was highlighted before.

**4.** Continue your entry by typing in **his is a text boc**.

**5.** Now the text area reads as shown below:

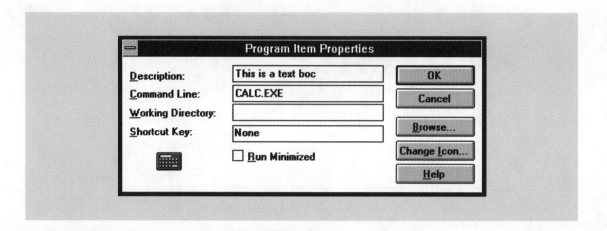

**6.** Oops! We've made a typo. Press **Backspace** one time, to erase the **c**. Now type in **x**.

**7.** Press ← three times. Notice that the text cursor moves to the left. Type **test**. The letters are inserted into the text at the location of the cursor, pushing **box** to the right. Press **Backspace**. Each press deletes a letter to the left of the cursor. Now you know how to position the text cursor to any location you want.

**8.** Cancel the box (and the changes you've made) by clicking the **Cancel** button.

Now you've tried out much of what you need to know to run almost any Windows program—believe it or not. Let's recap. You know how to:

- **Run** a program from an icon,

- **Size** and **move** the resulting windows,

- **Open** a program's menus,

- **Adjust** settings in dialog boxes, and

- **Enter** and **edit** text.

Even though we haven't experimented with any complicated programs, you actually know most of what's going to be asked of you when you do. For example, you'll use many of the same text-editing techniques with a simple word processor such as Notepad or Write (supplied with Windows) as you will with a full-blown word processor like Word for Windows. And while the number of menus and the commands on them will vary from program to program, the menu techniques will be familiar to you.

Anything you don't already know will be pretty easy to pick up now that you know about clicking on objects and general mouse usage.

# Tool Bars

These days a lot of programs include *Tool bars*—graphical representations of your screen that you can click on to bypass choosing commands from the menus. It's just a time saver. For example, Lotus 1-2-3 for Windows has a toolbar like this:

**More and more programs have toolbars like this one in Lotus 1-2-3 for Windows.**

**As an example, clicking on this button caused the number in cell A1 to be formatted as currency.**

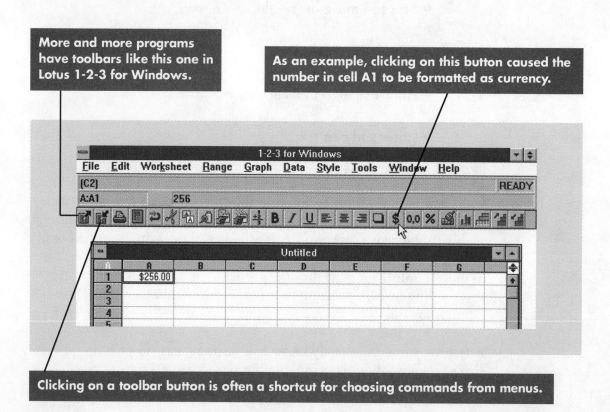

**Clicking on a toolbar button is often a shortcut for choosing commands from menus.**

**● Note** Programs such as WordPerfect or Lotus 1-2-3 have many of their own commands and their own peculiarities. A book on Windows will not explain these programs in detail—only those aspects that are common to all Windows programs. You'll need books written specifically about the other programs to learn more about them.

# Getting Help When You Need It

Regardless of what program you're running, there will be times when you don't remember or understand how to use an operation or command. Luckily, you don't always have to drag out a manual to get quick help. Windows programs almost always have a built-in Help feature that's pretty easy to use. With some better programs, including Windows itself, the Help will even be "context sensitive" — you'll get help about the specific task you're trying to complete.

The Help menu is always the menu farthest to the right. Try this:

1. From Program Manager, open the **Help** menu.

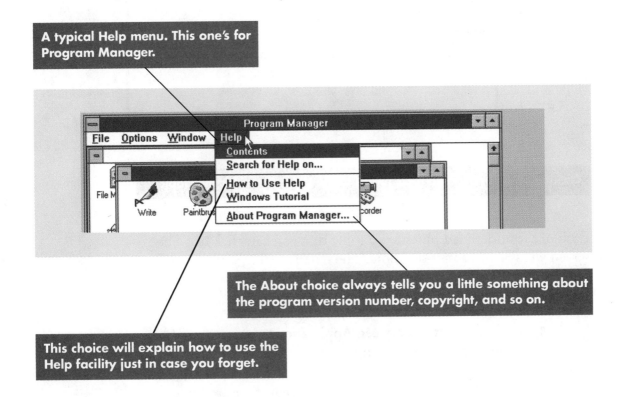

A typical Help menu. This one's for Program Manager.

The About choice always tells you a little something about the program version number, copyright, and so on.

This choice will explain how to use the Help facility just in case you forget.

**2.** Click on **Contents** to see a listing of all the Help items for a given program.

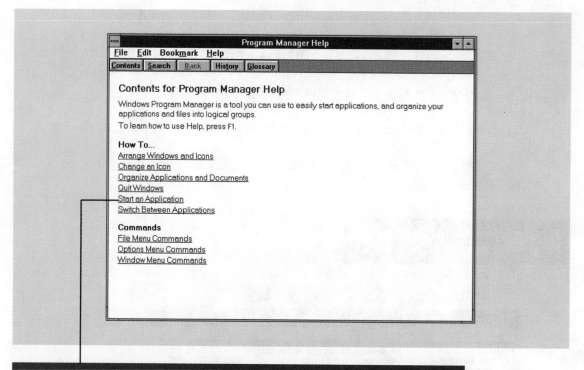

**Clicking on an underlined topic jumps to the Help screen for that topic.**

Each of the underlined phrases is a topic that you can click on. The screen will tell you about the topic. The next resulting screen may have more topics you can read about the same way—just by clicking on the topics you want. For example:

**1.** Click on **Switch Between Applications**. A screenful of help about that topic comes up.

**2.** If you have a color monitor, notice that there are some words that are highlighted in green and have dashes under them. (They look light gray if your monitor is black-and-white.) Clicking on these words will bring up a little box with a definition of the word in it. Click on the words **Control menu**, and up comes a little box containing a definition for that term:

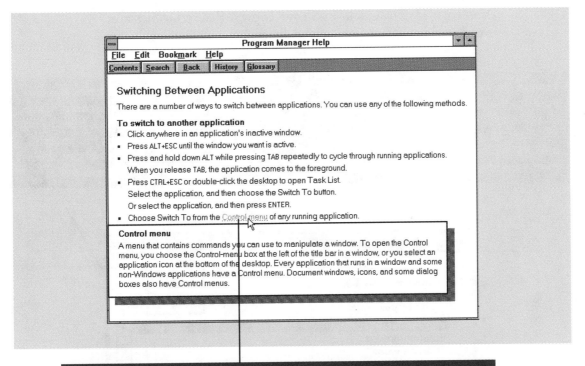

Clicking on a green, dotted-underlined word displays its definition.

**3.** Click again after you've read the definition, and it will disappear.

**4.** Click on the **Back** button. This takes you to the previous screen.

**5.** Now click on the **Search** button (just below the menu bar). This button lets you search for a topic about an application, even if it isn't listed on the Contents screen. It's a lot easier to use Search than to read all the Help screens in hope of finding the topic you want.

**6.** Now you see a list of available topics. You can scroll through them if you want, but there's a faster way. Suppose you want to know more about copying icons. Type in **copy**. The list quickly jumps to topics about copying, with *copying program items* highlighted. Click on **Show Topics**. Related topics are now listed in the bottom of the dialog box.

Type in the name of the item for which you want help. As you do, the list of topics below will jump to words with the closest spelling, attempting to guess what you're looking for. If nothing relevant comes up, backspace over the letters and try typing another word — like when you're looking things up in an encyclopedia.

Once you have the correct topic located in the top list, click here to narrow down the search topic. Results are shown in the bottom pane.

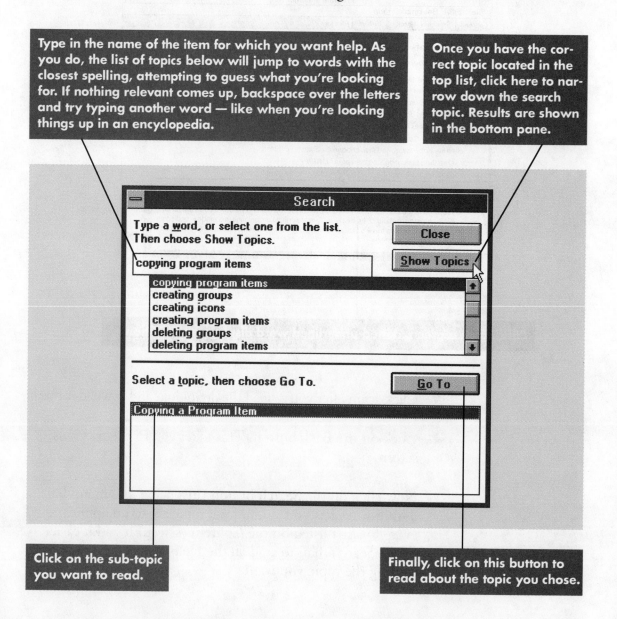

Click on the sub-topic you want to read.

Finally, click on this button to read about the topic you chose.

**7.** There's only one related topic for this entry and it's already highlighted, so just click on **Go To**. (If there were more than one, you'd click on the one you wanted to highlight and *then* on Go To.) Voilà! A screenful of help about Copying Program Items appears.

**8.** When you're through reading any Help file, regardless of the program, it's best to close the window, unless you intend to use Help a lot. (Your computer will have more available memory for other programs if you do.) Open the **Help** Window's **File** menu and choose **Exit**.

You can do a lot more with Help, but I'll spare you the details so we can get on to other things. If you want to explore Help, open the Program Manager's Help menu, choose How to Use Help, and follow the instructions.

Now turn to the next lesson to learn about switching between applications.

# Switching between Applications

One of the big attractions of Windows is that it lets you run several programs at one time and quickly switch between them. This means you can easily copy material between programs and documents, and you don't have to close down one job to start up another.

So far we've run only one program at a time—the Calculator program.

In this lesson, we'll experiment with running several programs and switching between them.

## Running Several Programs Simultaneously

The first step is to get several programs running. Just follow these steps to get a few of the Accessories programs running.

1. From the **Program Manager**, open the **Accessories** group window.

2. Double-click on the **Notepad** icon to run Notepad—a little program for jotting down notes. (If you don't see Notepad, click on the scroll buttons until it appears in the Accessories window.) An empty Notepad document opens, obscuring the Program Manager window at least partially, depending on the arrangement of your screen.

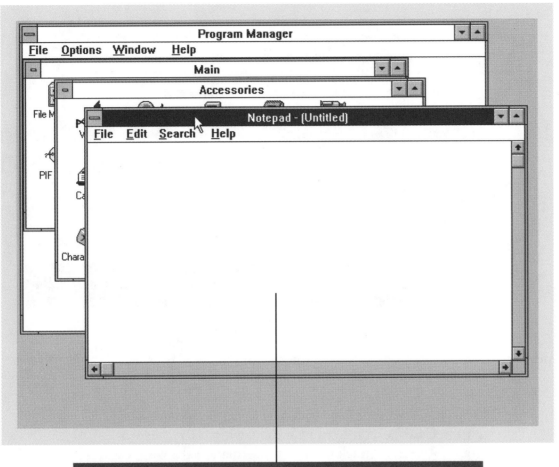

Any program you run will come up "on top" of other windows.

Hmmm. How do you get back to Program Manager to run another program?

**3.** You can probably still see part of the **Program Manager** window. Click on any part of it, even if it's just a corner, or the title bar. (If Program Manager is completely covered up, move or resize the Notepad window as you learned earlier until you can see a bit of the Program Manager window.)

*Quick&Easy*

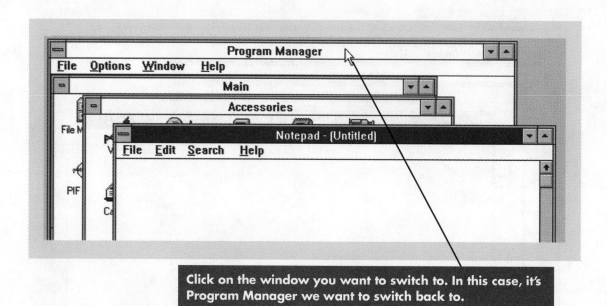

Click on the window you want to switch to. In this case, it's
Program Manager we want to switch back to.

Clicking on a window always causes it to "jump" to the front of all
other running programs. You can use this technique to get back to a
particular window as long as you can see a small piece of it.

**4.** With the Accessories window showing again, double-click
on the **Cardfile** icon to run Cardfile, which is a little program for keeping track of bits of information the way you
use a desktop Rolodex or index card box. A blank Cardfile
document now opens.

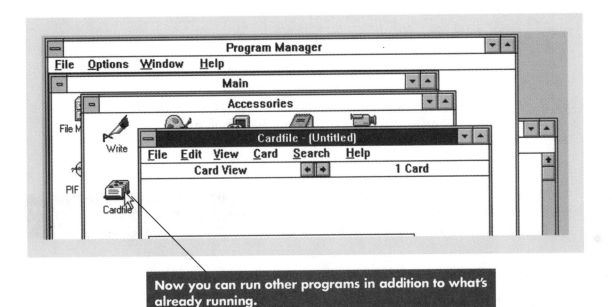

**Now you can run other programs in addition to what's already running.**

**5.** Click once again on some portion of the **Program Manager** window, and this time run **Calendar**. (Calendar is a program that helps you keep track of your appointments.)

## Switching between Programs by Clicking Their Windows

Now you have three programs running, right? Notepad, Cardfile, and Calendar, with Calendar on top. But consider this: although Windows lets you have several programs running at once, you can only be working or interacting with one program at a time—the *active* program. The others are waiting for you to get back to them. The question is how to switch between tasks—or between the windows you have on your screen. To see how this is done, try these steps using the three programs you already have in separate windows on your screen.

*Quick&Easy*

**1.** Click on the **Cardfile** window. It jumps to the front, covering most of the Calendar.

**2.** Click the title bar of another window to switch to that one. See if you can select the **Notepad** window. Is it in sight? If not, drag one of the other windows down so that you can see it, then click on it.

> When you have a lot of windows open at once, you may lose sight of some that are in back. Just drag the front windows down to redisplay the "lost" ones.

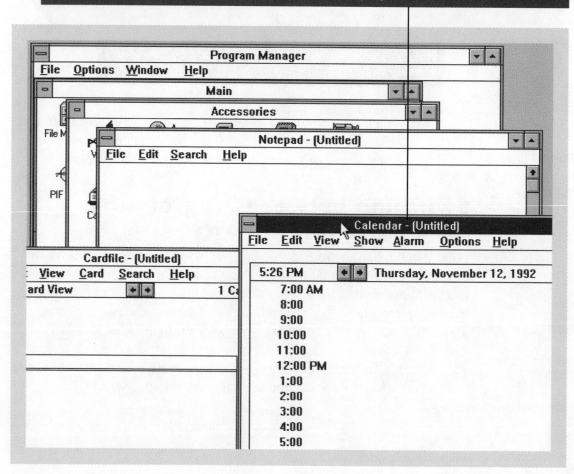

**3.** Try switching between windows by clicking anywhere within their perimeters.

## Switching between Programs by Using the Task List

By this point, things on your screen are pretty much a mess, aren't they? Including Program Manager, Notepad, Calendar, and Cardfile, you have about six windows on your screen. You may wonder if there is an easier way to switch between programs than trying to find an exposed corner to click on.

Luckily there is—with the *Task List*. The Task List lets you choose which of your running programs you want to jump to.

Here's how it works:

**1.** Press **Ctrl** and **Esc** (press and hold the Ctrl key while pressing the Esc key). This will bring up a dialog box called the Task List. The Task List shows you all the programs that are currently running.

**2.** You can easily switch to one of the programs simply by clicking on it and then clicking on the **Switch To** button.

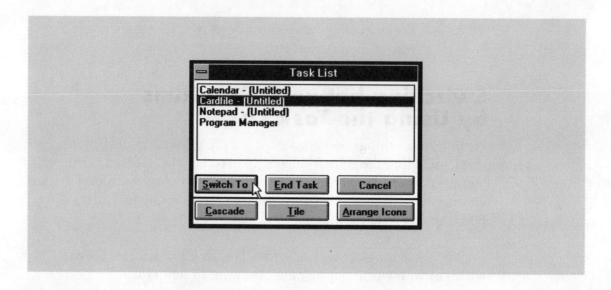

**● Note**  Don't be alarmed that Program Manager is included in this list.
The Program Manager is actually a program, too. While you're
in Windows, it's always running, and is necessary for
organizing your other programs.

Now try switching between programs from Task List:

**1.** Click on **Cardfile** to highlight it.

**2.** Click on the **Switch To** button (as you see above). The Card-file window comes to the top of the heap.

**3.** Press Ctrl and Esc to bring up the Task List once more. Click on **Calendar**, then on **Switch To**. Calendar now tops the pile of windows.

**● Note** You can switch tasks more quickly by double-clicking on the desired program in the Task List. This has the same effect as highlighting it and clicking on Switch To.

## Quickly Organizing Your Windows

You may have noticed some other buttons on the Task List. The two we're most interested in are *Tile* and *Cascade*. These two little numbers can help bring order from chaos when your desktop becomes cluttered.

Here are a couple of quick tricks for organizing your desktop:

**1.** Bring up the **Task List** again with Ctrl-Esc.

**2.** Click on **Tile**. This causes all the running program windows
to be arranged like this:

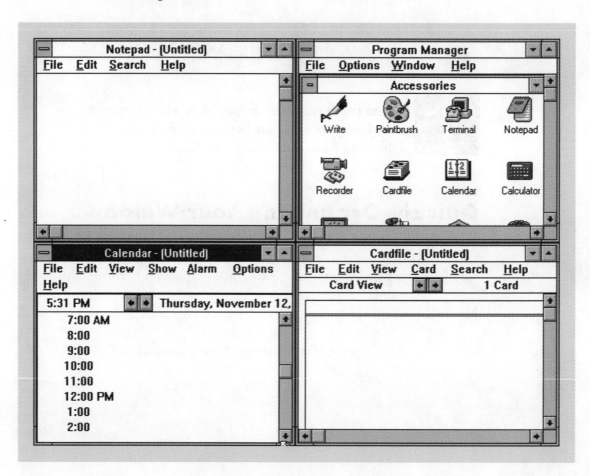

This arrangement is good when you need to see portions of all the
windows, or when you're referencing data in one window while entering
information into another.

**3.** Bring up the **Task List** again. This time click on **Cascade**. Your windows rearrange to look like this:

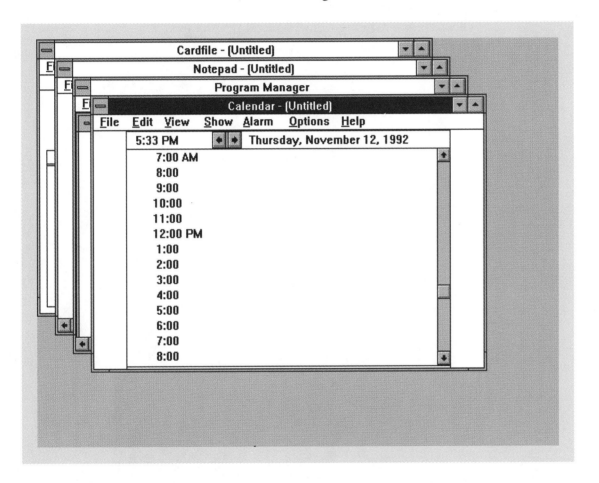

If your screen doesn't look like the picture, bring up the Task List and click on Cascade again. Depending on what windows are open, sometimes it takes two tries to cascade completely.

Now you can easily see the title bar for each program and click on it to bring it to the front, or enlarge it to full size it by clicking on its Maximize button.

**4.** Close both **Calendar** and **Cardfile** using the Control menus. If a little dialog box comes up asking you about saving changes, say No, since we didn't do anything you'd want to save. We're going to use Notepad in the next lesson, so leave that open.

# 8 Opening and Saving a Document File

As you now know, running a program, or even a bunch of programs, in Program Manager is as easy as clicking on icons. Once you have a program running, you'll often want to open up the files you create—whether a company budget, a collection of recipes, or a letter to your Uncle Frisbee, these are called *documents*.

## Storing Document Files

A document is a bit like the music on a tape in your cassette player. Without the tape, nothing happens—even if the machine is on.

As you may know, you store documents in your computer's internal memory, called the hard disk, or on a floppy disk so that when you turn off your computer, your work isn't lost. So, naturally, when you want to open the document again, you have to retrieve it from the disk.

In Windows, and with all Windows programs, you do this "retrieval thing" using the File menu's Open command. Similarly, when you've created a new document and want to save it, you use the File menu's Save command to tell Windows to save the document on disk.

In this lesson, you'll open an existing file that's already on your hard disk, and you'll save a new document file that you'll create.

> **● Note** Since we'll be working with directories in this lesson, I'll give you a brief overview of how they're used to organize your files. At the beginning of Lesson 14, I discuss directories in depth. If you want a more complete review before you proceed, look ahead to Lesson 14.

When you save files on floppy disks or on the hard disk in your computer, they're organized in *directories*. This is similar to a desk drawer or filing cabinet that has dividers of some sort to group similar files together. Within those divided sections, you might have folders where you keep related documents.

Let's say that in your top drawer you have dividers for each job you're working on, then separate file folders for invoices, letters, and progress reports. The top drawer is like your computer's *root directory*. The dividers and file folders are like *directories* and *subdirectories*, respectively. The individual files are your documents.

## Opening a File

Notepad should still be running after the last lesson. If its window isn't active, click anywhere in the window to activate it.

1. Open the **File** menu and choose **Open**.

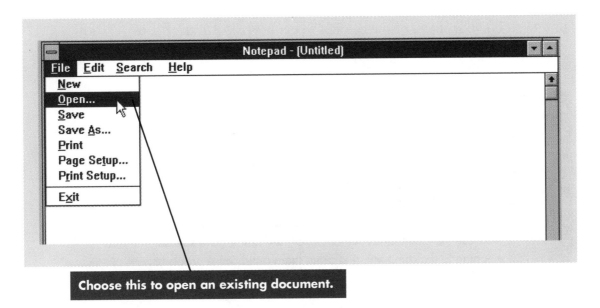

Choose this to open an existing document.

2. The **Open** dialog box pops up on your screen. This is perhaps the trickiest dialog box in Windows, but once you understand how it works, using it is a piece of cake.

To open a file, the object of the game is to get the name of the file to appear in the top left-hand box, the File Name text space. Then you click on OK. Simple enough? Let's do it.

> **• Note** Just a little reminder about file names, in case you've forgotten: All files on PCs have names of up to eight characters, followed by a period (.) and three more letters, like this: MYREPORT.TXT. You can use either uppercase or lowercase letters—it doesn't matter. You can use fewer letters if you want, and no extension, but it's best to use the extension that your program expects. For example, Notepad expects files to have .TXT extensions. DO NOT use the extensions .COM, .EXE or .BAT; these have special meaning to the computer, and using them could cause problems.

Since Notepad likes to edit files with an extension of .TXT, only .TXT files are showing in the left side of the dialog box. The asterisk before the extension .TXT in the file name space is called a wildcard and stands in for any file name. "*.TXT" means "any file ending with the extension .TXT." The extension is often referred to as the *file type*. SETUP.TXT is a text file supplied with Windows, so we'll use that as an example.

**1.** Click on the file name **setup.txt**.

**2.** Click on **OK**. The file is now opened, and loads into the Notepad window.

Notice that the title bar shows the name of the document you just opened, using its complete name, SETUP.TXT.

Notepad's title bar shows the name of the file that you opened.

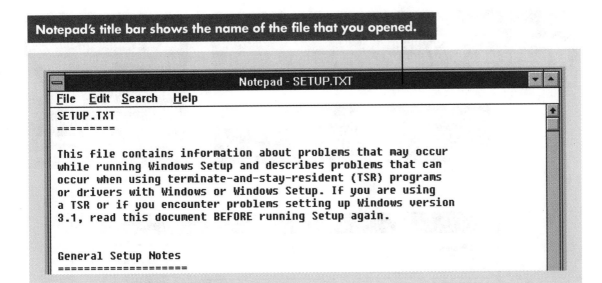

```
 ─                        Notepad - SETUP.TXT                    ▼ ▲
 File   Edit  Search  Help
 SETUP.TXT                                                          ↑
 =========

 This file contains information about problems that may occur
 while running Windows Setup and describes problems that can
 occur when using terminate-and-stay-resident (TSR) programs
 or drivers with Windows or Windows Setup. If you are using
 a TSR or if you encounter problems setting up Windows version
 3.1, read this document BEFORE running Setup again.


 General Setup Notes
 ====================
```

## Changing Directories

Good. Now you know how to open a document when its name is already showing in the list of files. Let's play with the Directory side of the file box for a minute so you can see how that works. You have to use the directory selector when the file you want is stored in another directory on your disk.

**1.** Open Notepad's **File** menu and choose **Open** again. (If you are asked about saving any changes you made, click on **No**.) The File box appears, just as before.

*Quick & Easy*

Type in the name of the document you want to open here, or type in a "wildcard" file name (such as *.TXT) followed by Enter to see a list of files whose names have a certain extension.

Use this box to open a file in a different directory. Double-click on the top line to back up one directory. Double-click on any directory folder to open it and display the names of the directory's files in the File name list.

Displays the directory (and subdirectory) location of the files currently showing in the File name list. This is the file's pathname.

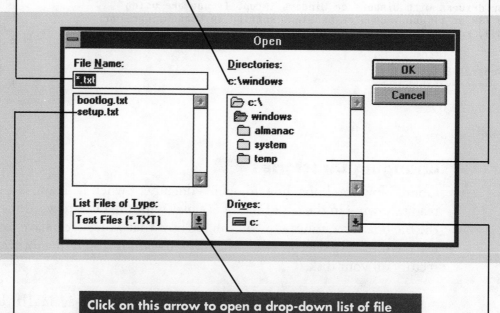

**Open**

File **N**ame:
*.txt

bootlog.txt
setup.txt

List Files of **T**ype:
Text Files [*.TXT]

**D**irectories:
c:\windows

c:\
windows
almanac
system
temp

Dri**v**es:
c:

OK

Cancel

Click on this arrow to open a drop-down list of file types. Only files that end with the extension you choose here will appear in the list of file names above.

You can choose the file you want to open by highlighting it here and then clicking on OK.

Click on this arrow to open a drop-down list of root directories, or disk drive letters, whose files you want to list.

**2.** Suppose you wanted to see what's on your computer's hard
disk. You'd double-click on the little **C:\** at the top of the
directories area. This C:\ is the root directory or drive letter, and designates your computer's hard disk. (A:\ and B:\
are also root directories and designate the floppy disk drives.)

---

**Double-click on the root directory to see all its directories listed below it.**

```
┌─────────────────────────────────────────────────────────┐
│ ▬                        Save As                         │
├─────────────────────────────────────────────────────────┤
│ File Name:              Directories:        ┌──────────┐ │
│ *.txt                   c:\                 │    OK    │ │
│                                             └──────────┘ │
│ ┌─────────────────┐▲    ┌─────────────────┐▲┌──────────┐ │
│ │                 │     │ 📂 c:\          │ │ │  Cancel  │ │
│ │                 │     │   📁 amarillo   │ │ └──────────┘ │
│ │                 │     │   📁 attitash   │ │            │
│ │                 │     │   📁 bats       │ │            │
│ │                 │     │   📁 beverly    │ │            │
│ │                 │▼    │   📁 collage    │ │            │
│ └─────────────────┘     │   📁 cursor     │▼│            │
│                         └─────────────────┘              │
│ Save File as Type:      Drives:                          │
│ │Text Files [*.TXT]│▼   │ ▭ c:           │▼              │
└─────────────────────────────────────────────────────────┘
```

The little file folder to the left of the directory name has changed color and
opened, indicating that C:\ is now the active directory. Of course, the directories listed below the root directory on your screen will be different from
those shown here, since your hard disk probably contains different directories than mine.

You probably don't have any files ending in .TXT in your root directory, so no files are likely to show up on the left side of the dialog box.
Nonetheless, you're back at the root level and you can double-click on
any of the directories in the right side of the dialog box to see if any
.TXT files are in them.

**3.** Let's move back into the Windows directory, then into a sub-directory of the Windows directory, the one called **system**. Double click on **windows** (if it's not showing, scroll the directory list first).

**4.** Now double-click on **system** and watch the directory list change. You've successfully switched directories several times now.

**5.** Move up one level by double-clicking on **windows**. You're back where you started.

## Saving a New File

Saving a new file—as opposed to opening an existing one—also relies on the File dialog box. The process is very similar. Let's create a small Notepad file and store it in the Windows directory.

**1.** Open the **File** menu and choose **New**.

**2.** If a dialog box asks whether you want to "save the changes" you've made, click on **No**.

**3.** Now type in a sentence or two about anything.

**4.** Open the **File** menu and choose **Save**. The **Save As** dialog box comes up.

**5.** You have to name the file and choose the directory. Notice that the file name is highlighted. This means that any text you type will replace the existing text. Type in **mytest.txt**.

Type in the name you want to give the file. The highlighted text (in this case *.TXT) will disappear, replaced by the file name you type.

Verify here that you've specified the correct location where your file will be saved.

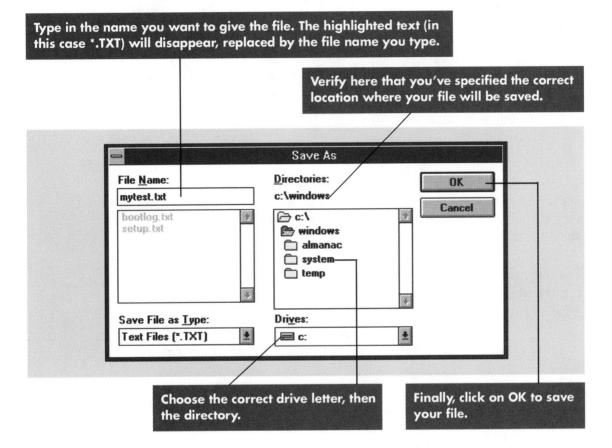

Choose the correct drive letter, then the directory.

Finally, click on OK to save your file.

6. Make sure you've selected the **Windows** directory. Look at the directory line just above the directory box. It should read **C:\windows**. (your drive letter may be different, like D: or E:, depending on how your computer system is set up.).

7. Click on **OK**. The file will be saved on your computer's hard disk. You can delete it later if you want. (You'll learn about deleting files in Part Three.)

5 MINUTES

# Printing in Windows

**Y**ou're very likely to want to print out "hard copies" of your work on paper. The exact procedure for printing may vary just a bit from program to program, but the steps are about the same for all Windows programs.

For our first experiment, we're going to print out the Notepad file you created in Lesson 8. If you closed Notepad after the last lesson, you'll need to run it and open the file you created. Follow these steps:

**1.** Double-click **Notepad** from Program Manager's **Accessories** group.

**2.** Open the **File** menu and choose **Open**.

**3.** Choose **mytest.txt** from the Open dialog box and click on **OK**.

OK. Now that the file's open, you can print it.

**1.** Turn on your printer. Make sure it's "on line," has paper in it, and is properly connected to your computer.

**2.** Open Notepad's **File** menu.

**3.** Choose **Print**.

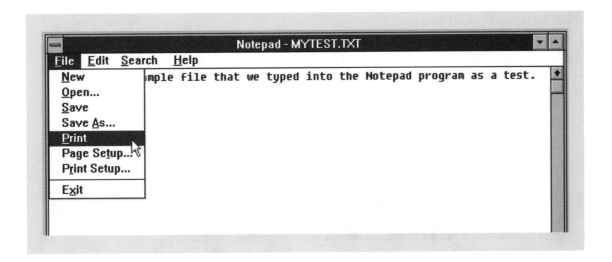

The following dialog box pops up, indicating that the file is being printed. Your printer should begin printing.

**4.** Close **Notepad**. We're finished with it for the time being.

## Setting Options for Printing

Though Notepad just went ahead and printed the document, some programs will let you choose which pages you want to print, the number of copies, and so on.

Here's an example to try:

**1.** In the **Main** window, double-click on the **Read Me** icon.

This runs the accessory program, Write, and loads a file called
README.WRI.

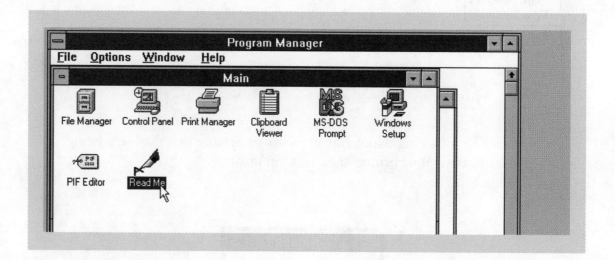

**2.** Open Write's **File** menu and choose **Print....**

You'll see a dialog box that gives you lots of options for controlling the
look of your printout, the number of pages to be printed, and so on.

When you print, you'll see a dialog box like this.

The name of the printer you're using appears here. If this is incorrect, click on Setup to change the printer name.

If you want to print some pages but not others, click on Pages and fill in the beginning and ending numbers of the pages you want to print.

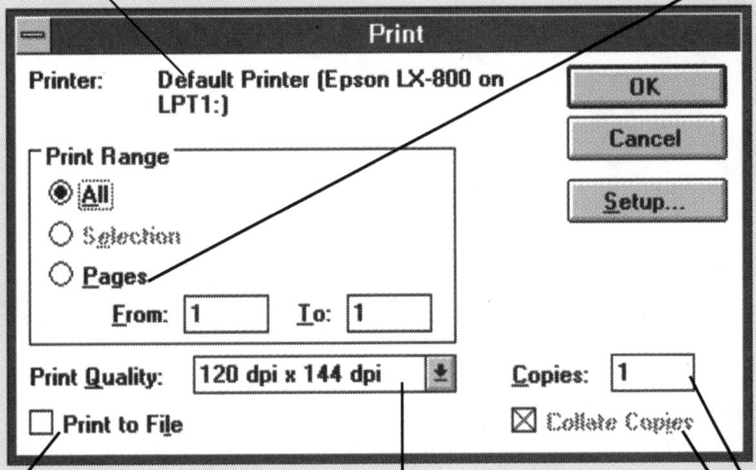

**Print**

Printer:   Default Printer (Epson LX-800 on LPT1:)

**OK**

**Cancel**

**Setup...**

Print Range
- ● All
- ○ Selection
- ○ Pages

From: 1    To: 1

Print Quality: 120 dpi x 144 dpi ▼    Copies: 1

☐ Print to File    ☒ Collate Copies

If you want to print to a file instead of to the printer, turn on this option. You can always print the file later.

With some printers, you can choose the print quality here. Lower print quality (*draft*) is faster.

If you print multiple copies, you can have them collated. This will, however, slow down laser printers.

**3.** Ready your printer again.

**4.** Click on **Cancel**. This particular file is over 25 pages long, so you probably don't want to print the whole thing.

**5.** Close the Document by opening the **File** menu and choosing **Exit**. If you accidentally made any changes to the file, you'll be asked about saving them. Click on **No**.

# 10

## Working with DOS from Windows

5 MINUTES

Thousands of programs were written for PCs before Windows was invented. These are called DOS programs, or DOS *applications*. Some examples are WordPerfect 5 for DOS, Lotus 1-2-3 release 2.2, and dBASE IV. There are many others. Windows versions of many DOS programs are becoming available, but you may not want to invest in them yet. Some perfectly good programs may never become available in Windows versions.

The good news is that you don't have to exit Windows to use DOS commands or programs. You use them within Windows, which is very convenient. You can even run several DOS programs at the same time and switch between them—just as you can do with Windows programs.

## Getting the DOS Prompt

Here's how you run DOS programs and use DOS commands with Windows:

1. Switch to **Program Manager**.

2. In the **Main** group window, locate the icon called **MS-DOS Prompt**.

*Quick&Easy*

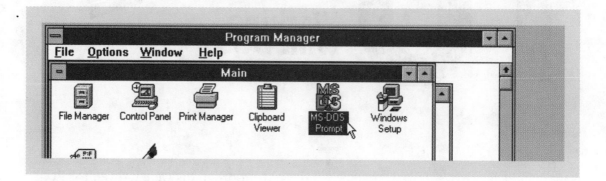

**3.** Double-click on the icon. This runs the DOS prompt. This
is called running a DOS "session."

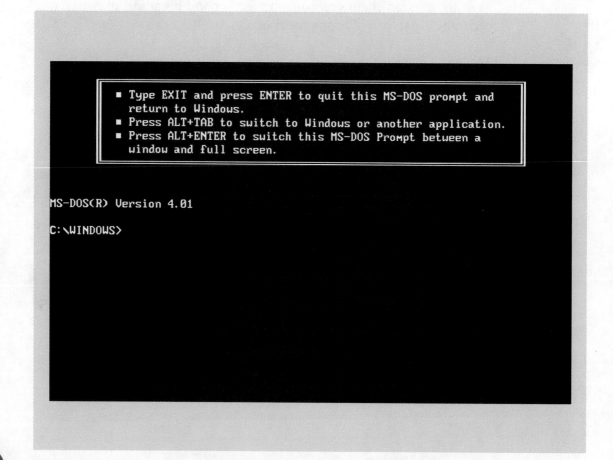

**4.** Now you can type in any DOS command. For example, to see a listing of all the files in the active directory, type **dir** and press Enter.

```
SYSTEM    INI      1693 08-10-92    3:20p
PROGMAN   02        302 02-12-92   11:02p
WIN       SYD      4570 01-18-93   10:20p
HOOKKM    DLL      8192 12-11-91   12:37p
PROGMAN   03        336 02-13-92    4:18a
VBRUN100  DLL    271264 05-10-91    1:00a
WIN       INI      5768 02-02-93    9:02a
T         TRM      4096 01-18-93    6:30p
CATALOG   CAT       620 06-02-92    4:21p
UNTITLED  CAT       258 05-22-92    1:36p
PHONEBK   CAT       258 05-30-92    2:17p
256COLOR  BMP      5078 03-10-92    3:10a
WINHELP   EXE    256192 03-10-92    3:10a
ARGYLE    BMP       630 03-10-92    3:10a
FLOCK     BMP      1630 03-10-92    3:10a
SSMARQUE  SCR     16896 03-10-92    3:10a
EMM386    EXE    110174 03-10-92    3:10a
DING      WAV     11598 03-10-92    3:10a
_DEFAULT  PIF       545 06-02-92    3:51p
BIOSXLAT  386     10088 01-09-91    1:18p
WINWORD   INI     11497 02-01-93    7:34a
ATTITASH  INI       503 02-13-92    4:01a
       156 File(s)     3405824 bytes free

C:\WINDOWS>
```

*Quick&Easy*

**5.** You can also run programs from your DOS prompt. For example, if you have dBASE III, you can start it up as usual and you'll see:

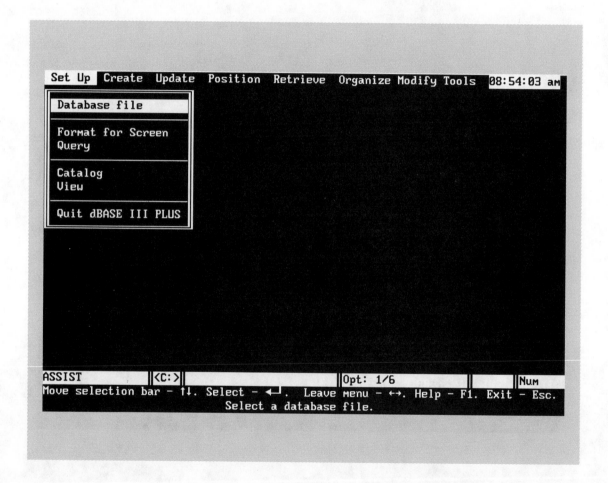

## Switching between DOS and Windows

Once you have DOS running, you can switch back to Windows without closing the DOS program. You could, say, be editing a document in WordPerfect for DOS, jump to Windows to check your calendar, and then jump back to WordPerfect. You could even run another DOS program by clicking the MS-DOS icon again.

Of course, you'll need to know how to switch between your DOS sessions and Windows. Let's switch back to Windows:

**1.** Press **Ctrl** and **Esc** to bring up the **Task List**.

**Choose Program Manager or another Windows program to get back into Windows.**

**2.** Notice the choice called **MS-DOS Prompt**. This is the DOS session.

**3.** Choose **Program Manager** and click on **Switch To**. Program Manager returns.

**4.** Return to the DOS session by opening the **Task List** again and switching to **MS-DOS Prompt**.

## Running DOS in a Window

If you have at least a 386 computer and 2 megabytes (MB) of RAM, you might be able to run DOS sessions in a window as well as full-screen. That way you can see other things you're doing in Windows, and you can then switch between tasks simply by clicking on the window you want to activate, rather than switching via the Task List.

**1.** Get to the DOS session. (It must be the active window.)

**2.** Press Alt and Enter. If your computer can do it, the screen will change to look something like this:

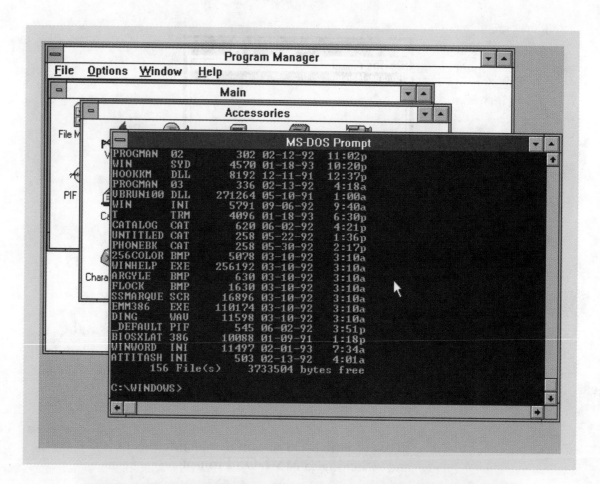

You can run DOS in a window if you press Alt and Enter. This only works if Windows is running in 386-Enhanced mode.

> **● Note** If nothing happens when you press **Alt** and **Enter**, your computer isn't capable of windowing DOS sessions.

**3.** Press **Alt** and **Enter** again to return to full-screen.

## Quitting a DOS Session

When you're through using a DOS session, you should close it. DOS sessions use up a lot of system memory and can slow down your system. Also, before you can exit Windows, you'll have to close any DOS sessions manually. If you don't, you'll see a message like this when you try to exit Windows:

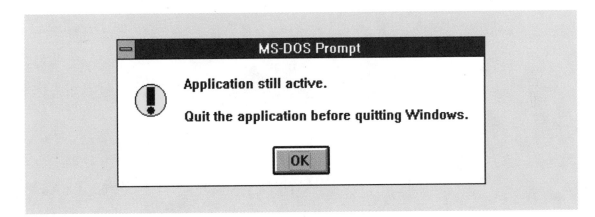

**1.** Click on **OK**, then switch to the DOS session.

**2.** Get back to the DOS prompt (**C:\>** by itself or with a directory name after it, like C:\WINDOWS>.) This might require closing the program you're running in DOS. For example, if you're using WordPerfect, press **F7**.

**3.** Once you're back to the DOS prompt, type **exit** and press
Enter. This closes the DOS session and returns you to
Windows.

**4.** Now try exiting Windows again. It should work this time.

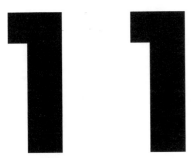

# 11

## Editing, Cutting, Copying, and Pasting

**10 MINUTES**

As you're writing a letter or entering data into a spreadsheet, you'll probably make a few mistakes in typing. Knowing how to use the Windows editing keys will make fixing "typos" easy.

Once you've perfected some text, it's also common to want to do a bit of rearranging, perhaps moving a paragraph or a sentence to another location. Commands on the Edit menu make this possible. You can edit text and then move it around from place to place, either within a document or between two diffferent documents. Here's how.

## Basic Editing Know-How

Actually, text editing is pretty simple. You have already used **Backspace** in earlier lessons, so you know the simplest editing trick. But there are a few others worth knowing.

For this experiment, we're going to use the Notepad.

1. Get to the **Program Manager**.

2. In the **Accessories** group, find the **Notepad** icon and double-click on it.

**3.** Type the sentence you see in the picture below, with the intentional error:

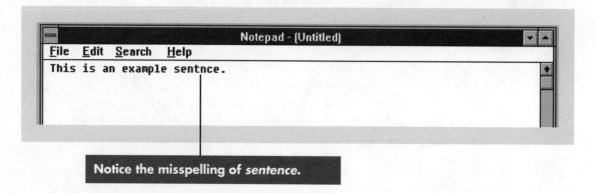

Notice the misspelling of *sentence.*

**4.** Let's fix the spelling error. Press ← (the left arrow, *not* the backspace key) several times to back up the blinking cursor until it's just between **t** and the **n** of **sentnce**.

**5.** Type the letter **e**. The end of the sentence is pushed to the right and the **e** is inserted.

OK. That's how you insert text. Just use the arrow keys to get where you want to go. Then type as much as you want. You could insert whole paragraphs or even pages.

Here's another approach:

**1.** Move the mouse. Notice that the cursor isn't the pointer any more. When you're editing text, the cursor often changes to this new shape called an *I-beam.*

**2.** Position the mouse cursor just before the **e** in **example**, as you see below.

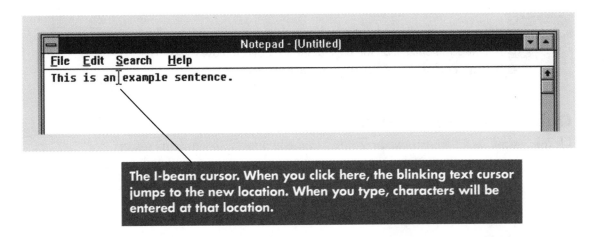

The I-beam cursor. When you click here, the blinking text cursor jumps to the new location. When you type, characters will be entered at that location.

**3.** Click once. The blinking text cursor now repositions. Repositioning the cursor this way saves you time when you're moving around in large documents.

**4.** Type in **appended**, and a blank space.

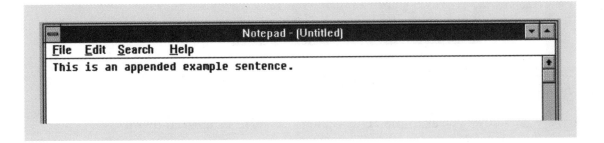

**5.** With the cursor just before the word **example**, press Del about eight times. With each press, one character to the right of the cursor is gobbled up. Get it? Backspace gobbles to the left, Del gobbles to the right.

**● Note** When you are editing documents larger than one screenful, you'll see the scroll buttons on the edge of the window. You use these buttons, or **PgUp** and **PgDn**, to move from page to page.

## Quickly Selecting a Word

Here's a time saver that most programs make available so you can select a single word quickly.

**1.** Position the I-beam cursor over the word **sentence** and double-click.

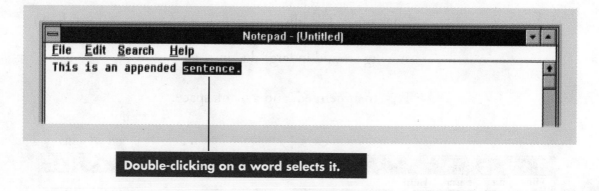

Double-clicking on a word selects it.

The whole word becomes selected in an instant.

**2.** Now type **example**. The highlighted word is replaced by the new word.

## Selecting Text by Dragging

Often you'll want to select more than one word at a time. To do this, you use the dragging technique you experimented with in an earlier lesson.

**1.** Position the I-beam at the beginning of **is**.

**2.** Hold down the mouse button and drag to the right, selecting **is an appended**.

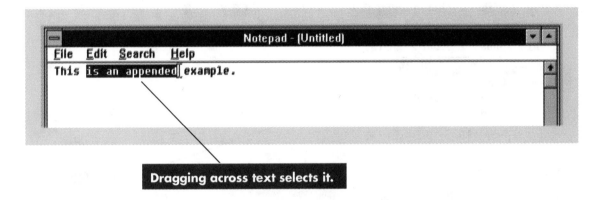

Dragging across text selects it.

**3.** Release the mouse button.

Just as before, if you press **Del**, the selection will disappear. If you type something, even a space, that will replace the selection. If you press an arrow key, or click the mouse, the words will be "deselected." For the time being, leave the words as you found them. We'll use them in the next section.

## Cutting, Copying, and Pasting

When you want to move material around, you have to follow three steps: First you select the material. Then you either *Cut* or *Copy* it, depending on whether you want to leave the original in place. Finally, you position the cursor where you want it to go and *Paste* it into the new location.

Here's an example. Let's use these commands to modify the sentence to read *This example is appended.*

**1.** The words **is an appended** are still selected from the last section.

**2.** Open the **Edit** menu.

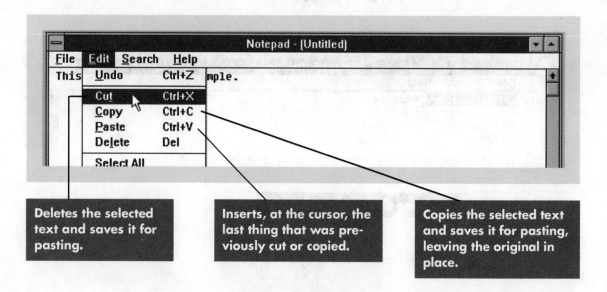

Deletes the selected text and saves it for pasting.

Inserts, at the cursor, the last thing that was previously cut or copied.

Copies the selected text and saves it for pasting, leaving the original in place.

**3.** Choose **Cut**. The words disappear. Actually, they are placed in a temporary holding tank called the *Clipboard*, where they can be used for pasting by Notepad or any other Windows program.

**4.** Remove any extra spaces between the two remaining words.

**5.** Move the blinking cursor to the end of the line using →
or the mouse (if you use the mouse, don't forget to click).
Put the cursor just before the period. You can adjust the
position after clicking by using ← and →.

**6.** Open the **Edit** menu and choose **Paste**.

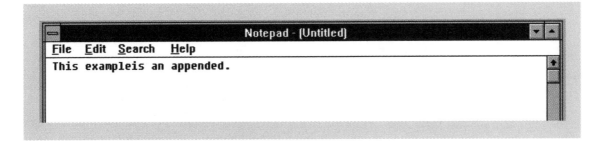

The text that was cut to the clipboard is pasted in at the cursor's location.

**7.** After pasting in material, you usually have to make some
adjustments. For example, notice the missing space between
**example** and **is**. Correct this by inserting a space there.

**8.** Now double-click on **an** to select that word. Press Del to
delete it.

Now the sentence reads correctly: *This example is appended.*

## Copying

So much for Cut and Paste. *Copying* is great for sharing material between documents. A case in point: consider the task of creating a letter
to stockholders. Say you want to compose it from two sources—text
taken from your company's promotional material, and graphs and fig-
ures from an annual profit-and-loss spreadsheet. No problem, *if* the

material is all in Windows programs. You use the *Copy* and *Paste* commands to copy material from each source document window and paste it into the destination window.

**● Note** Many Windows programs can import information from DOS programs, too. Check the program's manuals to find out how to do this.

Let's copy some text within our Notepad document, then copy something from Notepad into another program—Cardfile.

**1.** Select all the text in our sentence.

**2.** Open the **Edit** menu and choose **Copy**.

**3.** Now place the cursor at the end of the sentence (after the period) and press **Enter**. This creates a new line and moves the text cursor down to where you'll paste.

**4.** With the text on the new line, open the **Edit** menu and choose **Paste**.

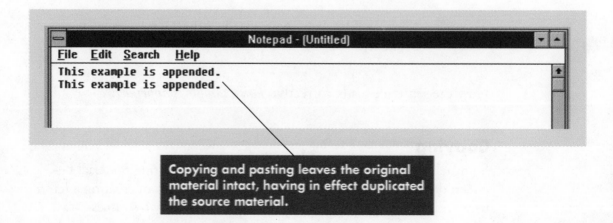

Copying and pasting leaves the original material intact, having in effect duplicated the source material.

You've just duplicated text without typing it in again. This can save a lot of time when you have to type headings throughout a document, "boilerplate" letters, or other repeated material.

## Copying between Documents

So far you've only done cutting and copying within the same document. Copying between different documents works in essentially the same way.

Try this to copy our sentence into a second, separate document:

**1.** Get back to **Program Manager** using the Task List (**Ctrl-Esc**, remember).

**2.** From the **Accessories** group, double-click on the **Cardfile** icon. A new Cardfile document opens.

**3.** Since the desktop is getting a little cluttered, open the Task List again and cascade the windows. Then arrange the Notepad and Cardfile windows as they are below so you can move between them easily.

**4.** Activate the **Cardfile** window, and open the **Edit** menu.

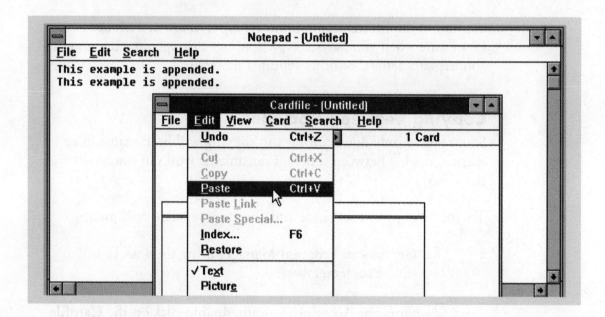

**5.** Choose **Paste**.

The same text you copied in the Notepad document is now pasted
into the Cardfile document, even though these two programs are very
different. Of course, you could have copied between two Notepad files
as well.

● **Note** You may have noticed that Cardfile's Edit menu has an option
for Picture. Many programs can share pictures (graphics) as
well as text. Even sound can be copied and pasted. See the
lesson on Paintbrush in Part Four for more about graphics.

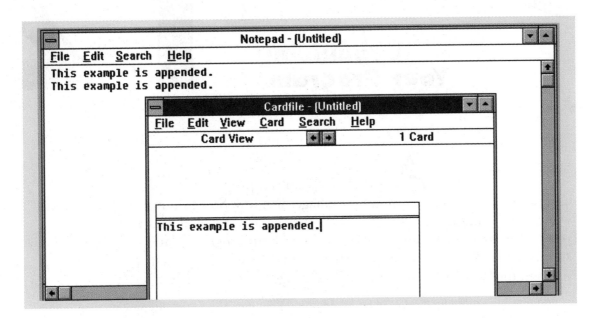

**• Note**  Remember that each time you cut or copy, the material on the Clipboard is replaced by the newly cut or copied material. Only one thing can be on the Clipboard at a time, so you have to do things in the correct order if they are to work—Copy, Paste; Copy, Paste; *not* Copy, Copy; Paste, Paste.

## Closing Up Shop

Let's tidy up before the next lesson.

**1.** Close Cardfile. Don't save the changes.

**2.** Close Notepad. Don't save the changes here either.

# Organizing Your Programs

# 12

As you know, you run programs by clicking on the icons stored in the Program Manager window. Still, you may wonder just what those icons are, where they come from, and what else you can do with them. There's a lot to know about Program Manager and its icons. But rather than overwhelm you with details, I'll first run through the basics: how to organize your programs for easier access.

## Moving Icons Around

First a brief recap. There are three types of icons:

- **Group** icons, which represent a group of similar programs or files gathered together.

- **Program** icons, which represent programs you can run.

- **Minimized** Program icons, which represent programs that are still running, but shrunken conveniently out of your way while you do something else.

Programs you can run are inside a group window.

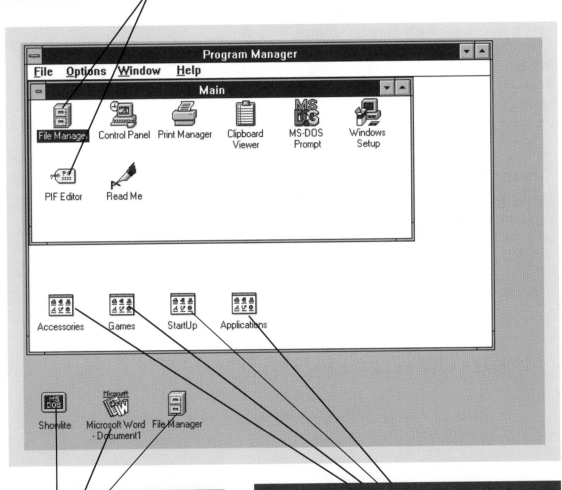

Program Manager

File    Options    Window    Help

Main

File Manager    Control Panel    Print Manager    Clipboard Viewer    MS-DOS Prompt    Windows Setup

PIF Editor    Read Me

Accessories    Games    StartUp    Applications

Showlite    Microsoft Word - Document1    File Manager

Programs that are running but minimized, sitting on the desktop.

Group icons represent a collection of programs. Double-click on each to open it up and see what programs are inside. Group icons are meant to organize your programs into categories that make sense to you.

You could have all programs in one group window, but that wouldn't help you organize them. When you installed Windows, it looked around your hard disk and made icons for popular programs you may have had, placing them in the Applications group.

When you install new programs, often a new group will be set up to include associated programs. For example, Lotus 1-2-3 for Windows creates a new group called Lotus and puts into the group a couple of program icons.

## Creating a New Group

Maybe you always use the same programs, and you want to put them in the same group for easier access. Or perhaps several different people use your computer, and you want to create a separate group for each of them.

Let's create a new group.

**1.** Get to **Program Manager**.

**2.** Open the **File** menu and choose **New**.

**3.** Make sure **Program Group** is the selected option, and click on **OK**.

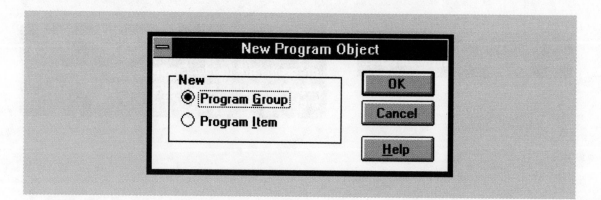

**4.** In the resulting dialog box, type in **My New Group**. You don't have to fill in the bottom line.

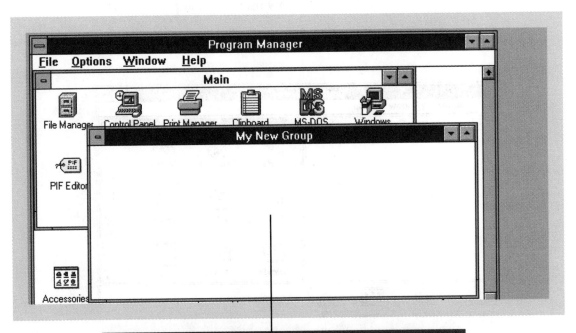

**5.** Click on **OK**. A new group is created.

The new group comes up empty when you first create it.

## Putting Icons in Your New Group

Let's say you want to put a couple of icons into your new group. You can move them, or you can copy them. First we'll move an icon, then copy one. Moving relocates an icon, whereas copying leaves the original where it was and puts a copy in the new group.

**1.** Open up the **Accessories** group window, or if it's already open, activate it by either clicking on a portion of its window or by opening the Window menu and choosing Accessories.

**2.** Now adjust the two windows so you can easily see them. Close any others that are open by clicking on their Minimize buttons.

**3.** Now, with two group windows open, you can really tidy things up by opening the **Window** menu and choosing **Tile**. The result is something like this:

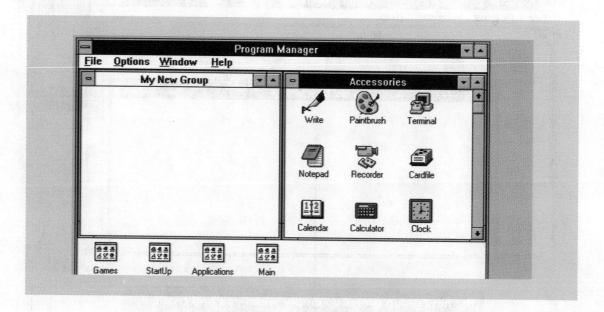

**4.** OK. Let's say you want to move **Notepad** into your new group. Simply drag it into the **My New Group** window.

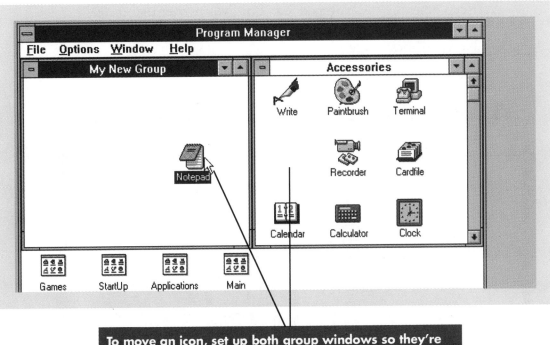

To move an icon, set up both group windows so they're visible, then drag the icon into the destination window.

**5.** Now move **Cardfile** over the same way. You've got two icons in the new group.

## Making Copies of Icons

What if someone else uses your computer and expects to find the Cardfile and Notepad accessories in the Accessories group? You'd better make copies of the icons to put back into their customary location. Here's how to copy icons:

**1.** Press **Ctrl** and hold it down.

**2.** Drag the **Notepad** icon back to the **Accessories** group window. As you do, a blank copy of the Notepad icon appears.

**3.** Keep dragging the **Notepad** icon until you're over the **Accessories** window, then release the mouse button. A copy of Notepad goes in the window.

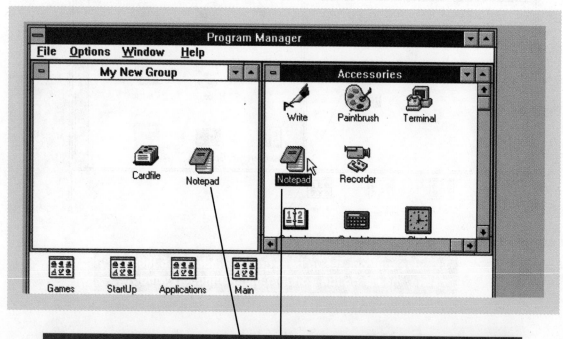

To copy an icon, hold down **Ctrl** and drag the icon to the destination group.

**● Note** Copying icons doesn't copy the program, only its representative icon, so you don't have to worry about wasting disk space by copying lots of program icons.

**4.** Now place a copy of the **Cardfile** icon back in the **Accessories** window.

# Keeping Your Icons in Line

After dragging and copying icons, or even just resizing group windows, your icons will get scattered about and misaligned. Here's how to tidy things up:

1. Click somewhere inside the window whose icons you want to straighten.

2. Open the Program Manager's **Window** menu and choose **Arrange Icons**.

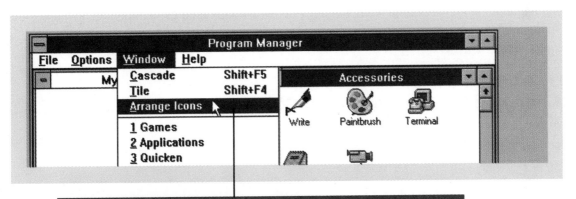

To arrange the icons neatly in a window, choose this command.

**• Note** If you want the icons to arrange neatly every time you resize any group window, open the Options menu and turn on Auto Arrange (a check mark will appear next to the command on the menu when Auto Arrange is on).

# Starting Up Programs Automatically

One last feature of the Program Manager and icons is worth mention-ing—the StartUp group. Any icons you add to this group will be run automatically whenever you start Windows. This is a great feature, and very handy if you tend to use the same programs day in and day out.

For example, I have File Manager, Notepad, Clock, and Microsoft Word in my StartUp group. When I start up Windows, all these pro-grams also start. I'm then ready to roll without even having to double-click on any program icons.

To use this convenience, just drag copies of your most-used programs into the StartUp group's window. Next time you start Windows, the programs will run.

## Changing the StartUp Group Contents

You can change the automatic StartUp group programs any time by deleting the icons or dragging them into another group. (This works with any group window, not just StartUp.)

Here's how you delete a program icon:

**1.** Highlight the icon in its group window by clicking on it once.

**2.** Press **Del**.

**3.** Answer **Yes** to the resulting dialog box.

**● Note** Though you can delete a group icon the same way, be careful, because all the *program icons* in the group will be erased along with it. Group icons are harder to get back than program icons, once they're deleted. Also—deleting a program icon doesn't delete the program itself, only its representation. You can always get the icon back by adding a program icon to the group window.

Congratulations! Now you're proficient at running programs and switching between them, printing, working with Program Manager windows, using icons, using menus and dialog boxes, and editing text.

Move on to the next section to learn about the File Manager—the part of Windows that helps you organize your files, your hard disk, and your floppy disks.

# Keeping Track of Your Files

One of Windows' greatest features is the way it lets you easily manage (copy, move, delete, etc.) your documents graphically once you have saved them on disk. File Manager is the part of Windows that lets you accomplish this and a few other things too, like formatting floppy disks. File Manager alone is worth the price of Windows because it's now so much easier to manage your files than it was with DOS. Part Three of this book explains all you'll need to know about File Manager for everyday use.

5 MINUTES

# Working with File Manager

# 13

We've already discussed the File dialog box used for saving and opening files, so you probably understand a very central concept about computers: your work is stored in "files" on your hard or floppy disks. When you turn off your computer, only the information you've stored on disk will be there when you turn on the computer again.

If you've worked with programs in DOS, you know what a hassle keeping track of your files can be. For example, you had to type *dir* to see where your files were. And you had to climb up and down directory trees to change directories if you couldn't find files where you thought they were. If you wanted to move or copy one or create a new directory to reorganize your files, you had to type commands on faith and hope that all your hard work wouldn't disappear forever.

File Manager lets you see your directories and files listed simultaneously. You can then move or copy them by dragging them around with the mouse, and you can rename or delete them by clicking on their icon, then giving a command or two. File Manager asks you to confirm your actions so you won't accidentally erase a file or copy over an existing one.

Now let's dig in and take a look at how File Manager works and what it can do for you.

# Getting to File Manager from Here

Windows comes from the factory with File Manager located in Program Manager's Main group, so this is where we'll look for it.

**1.** If the Main group isn't already open, double-click on the **Main** group icon.

**2.** Now double-click on the **File Manager** icon—the one that looks like a little filing cabinet.

Double-click on the File Manager icon in the Main group to open File Manager.

When the File Manager window opens up, it resembles the picture that follows (remember, yours may look different depending on what directories and documents you have and how things were arranged when you last left Windows).

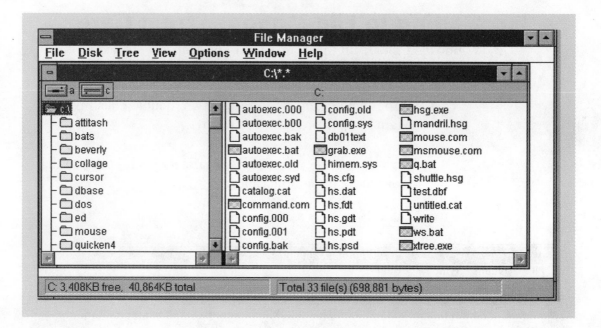

The remaining lessons in this section teach you how to use the features you see in the figure above. I'll explain them as you go along.

So turn the page and we'll get to it.

# 14

## Finding Your Way around Drives and Directories

15 MINUTES

Perhaps you don't know about directories, so I'll start off by explaining what they are first. Then you'll get to try your hand at moving around between drives and directories in File Manager. Once you're comfortable with that, you'll become adept at creating new directories, and moving and copying files between drives and directories, without ever taking your eyes off them.

Directories are organized in a system that resembles a tree. The most basic level of the tree is called the *root*; the next level, *directories*, are the bigger branches; and the *subdirectories* are the smaller branches coming off the directories.

It makes sense, then, that File Manager uses what is called a *directory tree* to organize your files.

Although you may not realize it, the DOS prompt (something like C:\> on your computer screen) designates a directory. By default (if you don't specify another directory), your computer usually puts files in C:, which is the *root directory* on your hard disk. When you type A: or B: to save documents onto a floppy disk, you're putting them in the root directory on the floppy in drive A: or B: (even if all that means to you is that you're saving material on a floppy instead of in the computer).

The structure of directories is like a tree. Windows calls it a directory tree. The most basic level is called the root directory.

The first branch in the directory tree contains directories.

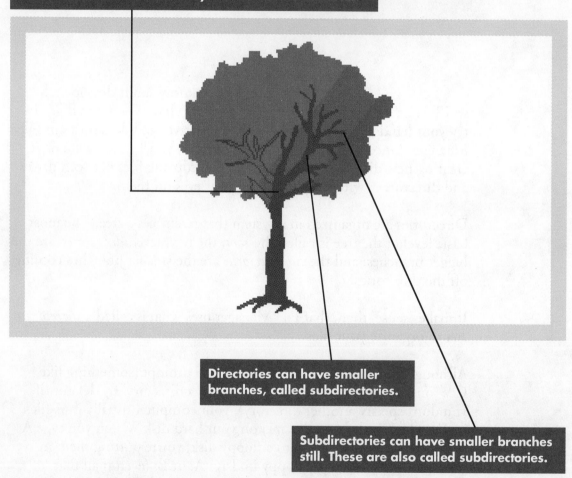

Directories can have smaller branches, called subdirectories.

Subdirectories can have smaller branches still. These are also called subdirectories.

Essentially, you use directories to group files or documents together when you store them. Directories are set up like your filing cabinet. The top drawer is the one you use most often and is the easiest to reach. That's like *C:*, your computer's root directory. Open up the drawer and the first thing you see is a Pendaflex (or some other hanging folder) for, say, the Acme Plumbing job. That's like a directory you might call *Acme*. Within the hanging folder you have separate manila files for invoices, correspondence, and progress reports. These files would be subdirectories you might name *Invoices*, *Letters*, and *Progress*. The different pieces of paper you put away in each manila file are your individual documents, or files.

With the explanations out of the way, let's get down to some practice.

## Viewing Files

Take a look at the *directory tree* pane (the left side of the directory window). Wouldn't it be easier to see everything if your directory window were bigger? Let's maximize it before we begin.

You'll want to maximize the File Manager window first, since it's the parent window and will limit the maximum size of the directory window.

1. Click on the **Maximize** button on the **File Manager** window's title bar. The window will expand to take up the whole screen.

2. Move the pointer to **C:\*.\***, on the directory window's title bar. The title bar tells you what's highlighted in the directory. Here it's C:, the root directory. To enlarge the directory window, click on the **Maximize** button at the end of the title bar. The directory window is as big as the screen now, and Restore buttons have replaced both the File Manager window and the directory window.

One directory window is always open in File Manager. It displays the contents of the root directory of the drive in use.

When you maximize the File Manager window, it takes up the whole screen, and the Maximize button becomes a Restore button.

Click on the directory window's Maximize button to enlarge it to fill the File Manager window (see the next picture).

The root directory (C:) is highlighted, and the right pane of the window, the directory contents pane, lists all the files in the C: directory.

The directory window's title bar shows you which directory is highlighted.

| File Manager |
|---|
| **File   Disk   Tree   View   Options   Window   Help** |

C:\*.*

C:

c:\
- attitash
- bats
- beverly
- collage
- cursor
- dbase
- dos
- ed
- mouse
- quicken4

| | | |
|---|---|---|
| autoexec.000 | config.old | hsg.exe |
| autoexec.b00 | config.sys | mandril.hsg |
| autoexec.bak | db01text | mouse.com |
| autoexec.bat | grab.exe | msmouse.com |
| autoexec.old | himem.sys | q.bat |
| autoexec.syd | hs.cfg | shuttle.hsg |
| catalog.cat | hs.dat | test.dbf |
| command.com | hs.fdt | untitled.cat |
| config.000 | hs.gdt | write |
| config.001 | hs.pdt | ws.bat |
| config.bak | hs.psd | xtree.exe |

The directory tree pane reveals the directory structure of the selected drive.

The directory contents pane lists the files in the directory that's highlighted in the directory tree pane.

Before you continue, take a look at the panes of the directory window. The left pane, the directory tree, shows the root directory (that *C:* I keep talking about) at the top of the list. This is often referred to as the *drive letter*. If you save your files into your computer, the drive letter is usually C:. If you save files on floppy disks, the drive letter you're used to is probably A: or B:, depending on the number of slots you have on your computer for floppy disks.

Branching off from C: in the picture, you see a list of words preceded by pictures of little folders. These are the names of directories on drive C:, and the *directory icons*. The right side of the window, the directory contents pane, contains another list of words preceded by icons. For now, don't concern yourself with what each one is. Instead, we'll switch to another directory.

## Switching from Directory to Directory

1. Move your mouse pointer to **Windows** near the bottom of the directory tree in the left pane and click. As you do, the directory name and icon will become highlighted, and you'll see the contents of the right pane change. You're watching File Manager update the screen to display the files in the Windows directory.

*Quick Easy*

The files in the directory contents pane are different from the ones you saw there when C:\ was highlighted.

Click on the word *windows* in the directory tree to list all the files stored in that directory.

When the directory window is maximized, the title bar shows the name of both windows—File Manager and the directory window C:, plus the name of the directory that's highlighted in the tree, in this case Windows.

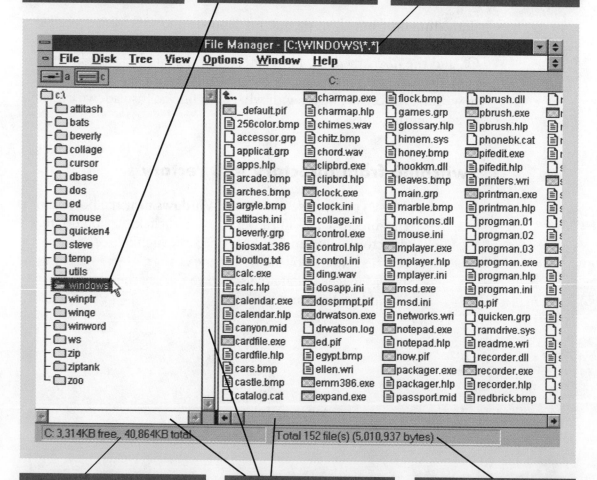

The status bar gives you helpful information about the root directory displayed. The left side tells you how much memory the directory has in total, and how much is still available.

Scroll bars in File Manager window panes allow you to move and see all the files in the directory when the pane isn't large enough to list them.

The right side tells you how many files there are in the highlighted directory, and how much memory they take up.

2. Click on another directory name to see the panes change again. Changing directories to see your files is as simple as that.

## Switching to See Files in Another Root Directory

Now we'll take a look at the contents of a root directory on another drive. Find a floppy disk that you've saved some documents on, or one that came with Windows. We're not going to do anything but look at it, so it doesn't matter what it is.

1. Insert the floppy disk in drive slot A:. (If you have two floppy drives, and the disk you're using will only fit in drive B:, go ahead and use that drive and substitute B: for A: in these directions.)

2. Position the mouse pointer on **A:**, and click. (Look at the picture below if you don't remember where the drive selector is. It's the icon above the root directory, with a little slot and the letter A: next to it.)

3. The root directory in the directory tree pane should now indicate the drive letter you just clicked, and the directory contents pane should list all the files in it. If you see something different, try again.

To change the display again, click on
another drive selector icon.

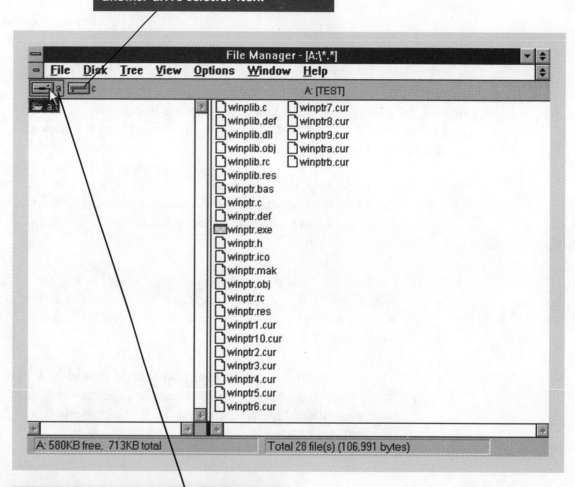

Click on the drive selector icon to replace
the contents of the directory window with
the files in another root directory.

A little caution here. Nothing serious, just that if you try to change the drive to see a file listing for a different directory but there isn't a floppy disk in the drive slot, you'll get an error message.

To proceed, insert a disk into the appropriate slot and click on Retry. If you change your mind or can't find the disk, click on Cancel.

**4.** Now switch back to your C: drive by clicking on the **C:** icon.

Oh, one more thing about the directory window—the View menu lets you adjust how much information File Manager lists for you. Look at the menu options in the picture that follows.

Change the sizes of the two panes. You might want more files in the contents pane so you can see them all at once without scrolling.

Choose how much information you see in the directory window—both sides, only the left side, or only the right side.

Choose how much information you want displayed in the contents pane by specifying the file details—name only, all information, or selected information.

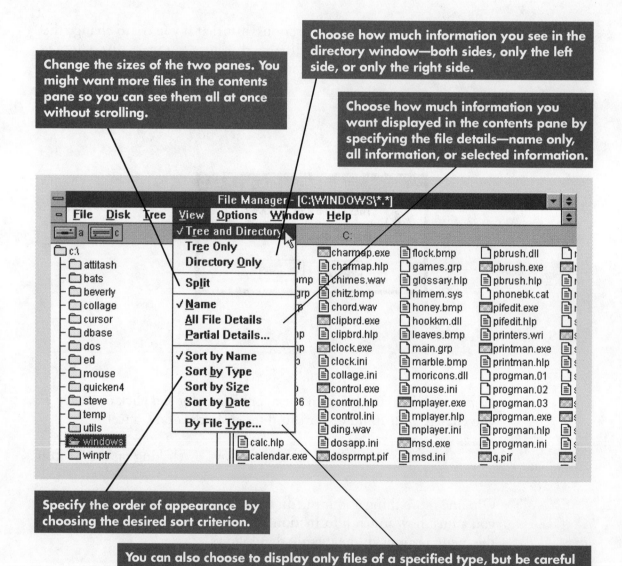

Specify the order of appearance by choosing the desired sort criterion.

You can also choose to display only files of a specified type, but be careful when you use this setting. If you forget to change it back to Display All File Types, you may think you've lost scads of files when in actuality they're just not included in the listing. Check this first if you're missing files.

You can set up your screen so that you see both panes of the window, or only one or the other. You can also adjust where the split falls between the two panes with the Size option. In addition, although right now the directory listing shows only the file names, you can change this by specifying which file details you want included. Finally, you can sort the files in different ways:

- **Name** sorts alphabetically by name.

- **Type** sorts alphabetically by file type (so that all files with the same three letters after the filename—called the file *extension*—are grouped together, then alphabetized within that group.

- **Size** sorts by size in megabytes(MB), with the smallest first.

- **Date** sorts by the last date the file was modified, with the most recent first.

These different settings can simplify your examination of the directory window if you're looking for files with certain similarities, or if you're looking for something in particular. Remember, though, that if you sort the files to an order you're not accustomed to using, you may overlook a file you need because it's not listed where you think it will be. Sorting by name is usually the best way to go until you're more comfortable navigating in the File Manager.

## Expanding and Collapsing the Directory Tree

Before you start working with the directory tree, there's a feature in File Manager that you need to turn on. First we'll turn it on. Then I'll tell you what it does.

1. Open the **Tree** menu.

2. Choose the **Indicate Expandable Branches** option.

The directory tree disappears for a few seconds, and when it returns, you see little plus signs in some of the directory icons.

```
┌─ 🗁 coreldrw          │ 🗋 dxfhead2.dat 🗋 impbmp.dll
│   ├─ 🗀 autoback       │ 🗋 expai.dll    🗋 impcgm.dll
│   ├─ ⊞ draw           │ 🗋 expat1.dll   🗋 impdxf.dll
│   ├─ 🗁 filters        │ 🗋 expbmp.dll   🗋 impgdf.dll
│   ├─ 🗀 fonts          │ 🗋 expcgm.dll   🗋 impgem.dll
│   └─ ⊞ photopnt       │ 🗋 expdxf.dll   🗋 impgif.dll
├─ 🗀 dos               │ 🗋 expgdf.dll   🗋 imphpgl.dll
```

Whenever you see a directory icon with a plus sign, File Manager is telling you the directory has at least one level of subdirectories within it, where files are collected together in still smaller groups to keep everything separate and organized.

Since the Windows directory icon has a plus sign in it, we'll use it to experiment with expanding and collapsing a directory.

**1.** Double-click on the **Windows** directory in the directory tree. It will expand to display its subdirectories. Notice that the plus sign in the directory icon changed to a minus sign. This tells you that the branch is expanded. Even though you expanded the directory, nothing in the contents pane changed. That's because the Windows directory is still highlighted. If you highlighted one of the subdirectories, you'd see the contents change. But don't do that yet.

**Double-click on the directory to expand the directory branch to show the subdirectories.**

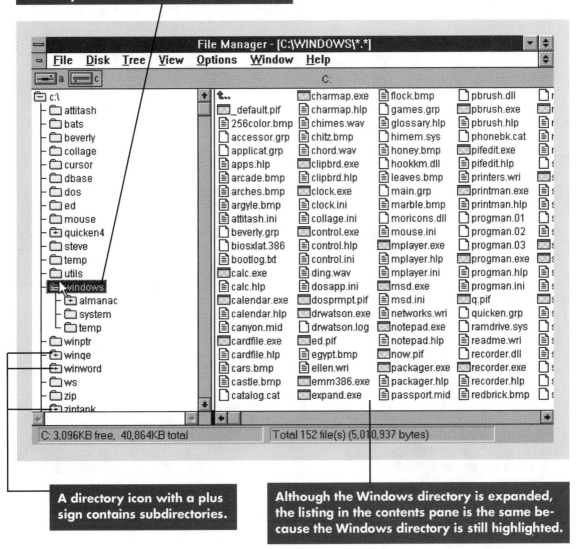

File Manager - [C:\WINDOWS\*.*]

**File   Disk   Tree   View   Options   Window   Help**

C:

**A directory icon with a plus sign contains subdirectories.**

**Although the Windows directory is expanded, the listing in the contents pane is the same because the Windows directory is still highlighted.**

Notice in the picture that the Almanac subdirectory has a plus sign. It must have a subdirectory, too.

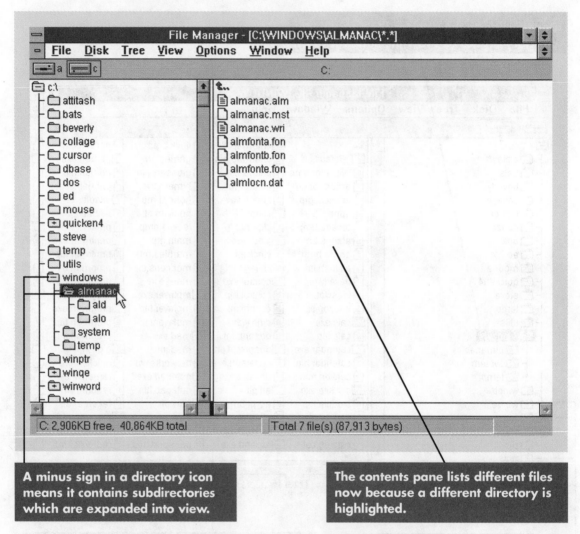

**A minus sign in a directory icon means it contains subdirectories which are expanded into view.**

**The contents pane lists different files now because a different directory is highlighted.**

**2.** Double-click on the **Windows** directory again. The branch will collapse, and the minus sign will change back to a plus sign.

Even when a directory is collapsed, you can still see the first branch of its subdirectories if you want to. Open the View menu and choose By File Type.... Directories will look like little folders over to the right in the contents pane. No matter how you sort your listing, directories always appear first in the list.

Here's one more thing to practice:

**3.** Go to the root directory at the top of the tree, either by clicking on **C:** or by pressing **Home**. Now double-click. The entire tree will collapse to show only the root—indicated by the drive letter.

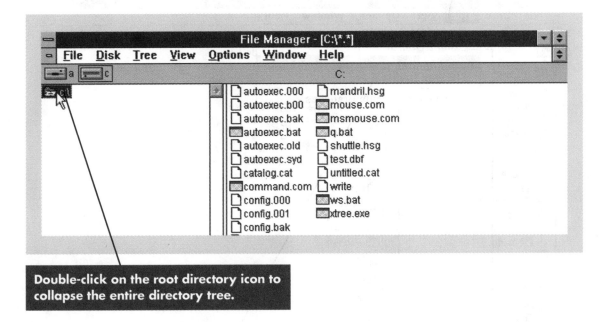

**Double-click on the root directory icon to collapse the entire directory tree.**

**4.** Double-click again to see the whole tree reappear.

**5.** Open the **Tree** menu again. The options here allow you to do pretty much what you just did by double-clicking, except you can expand all the branches of every directory with the Expand All option. Expand One Level lets you open the first level of subdirectories for every directory that has them.

**6.** Click on **Expand All** to see the new, expanded directory tree. You can now see all directory and subdirectory branches.

*Quick & Easy*

The Tree menu lets you expand the entire tree or expand and collapse branches (directories) individually.

Click on Expand One Level to show the next level of directories or subdirectories below the current level for the highlighted directory (If the root directory is highlighted, this expands the entire tree.)

File Manager - [C:\*.*]

**File   Disk   Tree   View   Options   Window   Help**

Expand One Level                +
Expand Branch                   *
Expand All              Ctrl+*
Collapse Branch                 -
√ Indicate Expandable Branches

a   c

c:\
├ attitash
├ bats
├ beverly
├ collage
├ cursor
├ dbase
├ dos
├ ed
├ mouse
├ quicken4
│  ├ bobquk91
│  ├ bobquk92
│  ├ charquik
│  └ martquik
├ steve
├ temp
├ utils
├ windows
│  ├ almanac
│  │  ├ ald
│  │  └ alo
│  ├ system
│  └ temp

dril.hsg
se.com
ouse.com

autoexec.syd          test.dbf
catalog.cat           untitled.cat
command.com           write
config.000            ws.bat
config.001            xtree.exe
config.bak
config.old
config.sys
db01text
grab.exe
himem.sys
hs.cfg
hs.dat
hs.fdt
hs.gdt
hs.pdt
hs.psd
hsg.exe
shuttle.hsg

C: 2,964KB free,  40,864KB total          Total 33 file(s) (698,881 bytes)

Expand Branch opens all levels of the highlighted directory.

Highlight an expanded directory and click on Collapse Branch to show less detail. You can collapse any level of an expanded directory to show as much or as little detail as you like.

While the Indicate Expandable Branches feature can be helpful, it does slow down the time it takes for Windows to update your directory listings. You may want to turn it off when you need to work faster.

With this lesson behind you, you should understand directories a bit better and have some basic navigational skills well under control. I want you to start enjoying one of File Manager's biggest assets, which is how simple it makes moving, copying, renaming, and deleting files.

Since Windows makes organizing related files into directories so easy, in the next lesson you'll learn how to create any directory structure that makes finding your files easiest for you. Then in the lesson after that, you'll learn how to copy files, move them around, rename them, and delete them. Read on—you're finally getting to the good part.

15 MINUTES

# Why You Need Directories, and How to Use Them

# 15

In this lesson you're going to learn how to make new directories that you can put files into so that similar documents are grouped together. The advantage of doing this is that when you can't remember what you named your letter to Aunt Martha or where you put it, if you have a directory called *Letters*, chances are it's in there. By opening the directory and looking at the file names, it shouldn't be too hard to find Aunt Martha's letter.

Then you'll learn to rename and delete directories, which will enable you to be more creative with your organizational structure. Finally, I'll teach you how to view several directories at once. This comes in handy when you want to move subdirectories or files from one place to another to tidy things up.

## Making a New Directory

First things first. Now that you've got the bug to organize your files, you need to make directories with descriptive names to put things into. Follow these steps:

1. We last left the File Manager with all its branches expanded, so let's collapse them again by double-clicking on the **C:\** at the top of the directory tree. Then double-click on the **C:\** again to show the first branch of directories.

2. We'll use the Windows directory for the purposes of this exercise. Click on **windows** in the directory tree to list its files in the contents pane.

**3.** Only about half of the Windows directory files show in the contents pane. You can tell because the scroll bar reminds you that the pane contains files you don't see. To display more of the files, we'll resize the panes. Place your mouse pointer over the border between the two panes. It will change to a double-headed arrow.

**4.** Press your mouse button down and drag the border to the left until it's almost even with the right side of the names in the directory tree.

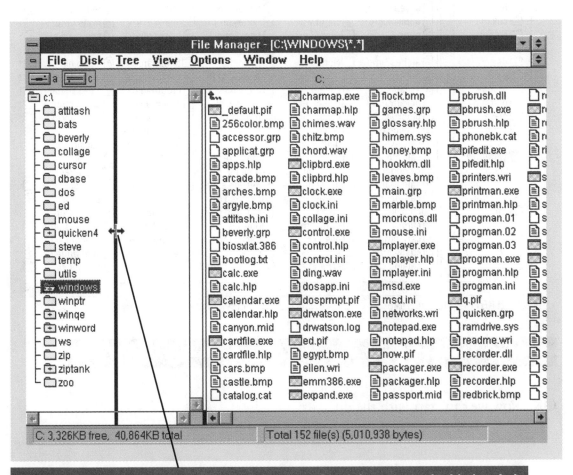

Place the mouse pointer over the pane's border. When it becomes a double-headed arrow, click and drag the border where you want it. Then release the mouse button.

**5.** Release the mouse button. The edge of the contents pane jumps to the left, and you can see a lot more of the files. (How many you see will depend on the size of your screen.)

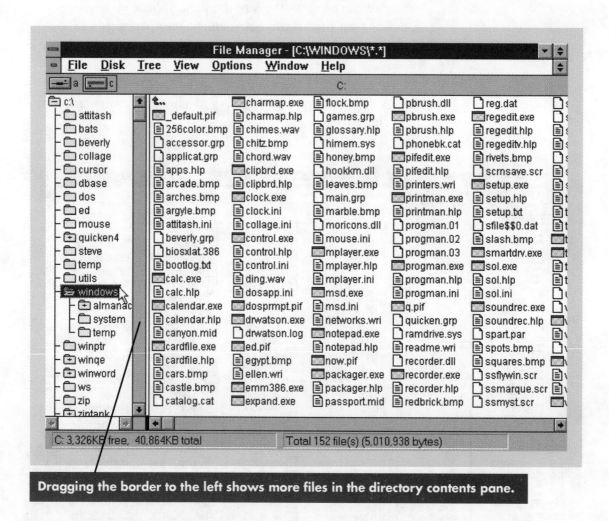

Dragging the border to the left shows more files in the directory contents pane.

OK. Now we can start with the directory exercises.

**6.** We want your new directory to branch off of the root directory, so the first step is to highlight the root by clicking on **C:\**.

**7.** Open the **File** menu and choose **Create Directory**.

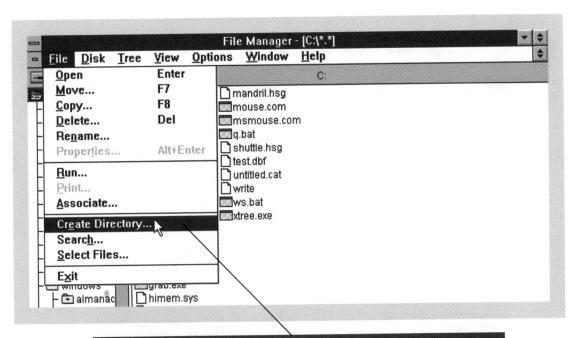

To create a new directory, highlight the directory where you want to place it, and click on Create Directory in the File menu.

**8.** A dialog box opens up, where you'll enter the directory name. For simplicity's sake, let's name it something that places it immediately under the root directory symbol. How about *aardvark*? Type **aardvark** in the dialog box.

**9.** Click on **OK**. The new directory will appear just below C:\.

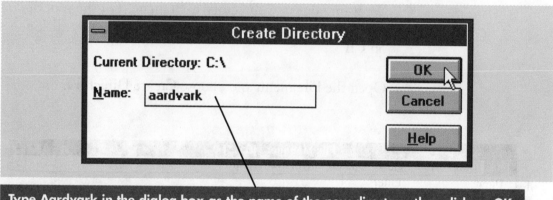

Type Aardvark in the dialog box as the name of the new directory, then click on OK.

**10.** Now create two more directories the same way. Call them **anteater** and **armadillo**. This way we have three harmless new directories to fool around with in the next few lessons.

When you're finished, the top of your directory tree should look something like the picture. Notice, though, that *armadillo* got cut off and only says *armadill*. That's because directory names can only have eight letters. *Armadill* is OK for now.

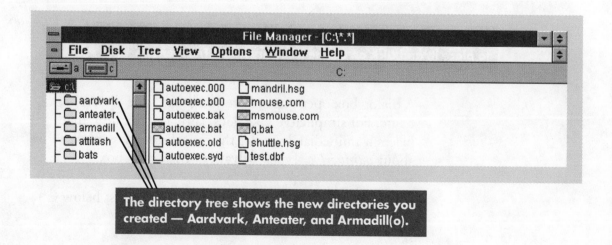

The directory tree shows the new directories you created — Aardvark, Anteater, and Armadill(o).

That's all there is to it—you know how to create new directories. If you want to create a subdirectory within a directory, just remember to highlight the directory first. When you create the subdirectory (just as you did above) it will automatically appear in the branch below the directory. If you forget to highlight the directory first and your subdirectory ends up somewhere else, you can move it. You'll learn how to do that in a minute, but first you'll delete one and rename one.

## Deleting a Directory

Sometimes after reorganizing your files you end up with an empty directory you want to get rid of. Or you might decide that it's dumb to keep all the letters you've written to Aunt Martha over the last six years. You can delete a directory whether or not it's empty. This is a little like throwing away a file folder or an envelope full of papers. When the folder goes, so do its contents. For this reason, Windows gives you two chances to reconsider. If you go ahead, the directory and all the files in it are gone, and I mean gone. But Windows does let you think about it before you take the plunge.

Let's try it. We'll delete the Anteater directory.

**1.** Click on **anteater** in the directory tree.

**2.** Press **Del**, or open the **File** menu and choose **Delete**.

**3.** Windows will give you your first chance to change your mind.

*Quick & Easy*

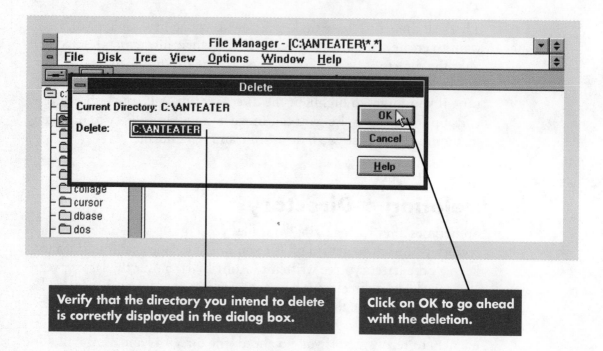

Verify that the directory you intend to delete is correctly displayed in the dialog box.

Click on OK to go ahead with the deletion.

**4.** The Delete dialog box shows you the name of the directory you have told Windows to delete. (If you change your mind, click on Cancel.) We're going to proceed, so click on **OK**.

**5.** Another dialog box pops up asking you to confirm that you really do want to delete that directory. You do, so click on **Yes**.

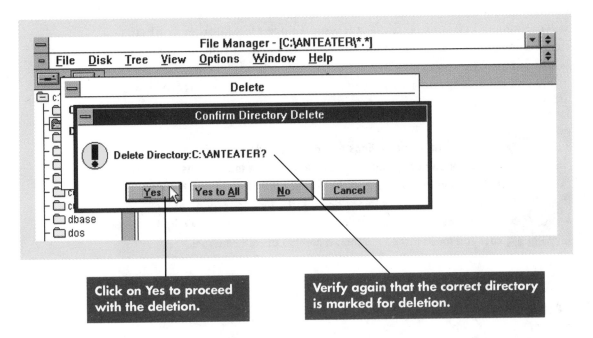

Click on Yes to proceed
with the deletion.

Verify again that the correct directory
is marked for deletion.

**6.** The directory is deleted. Look at the directory tree. Anteater
is gone.

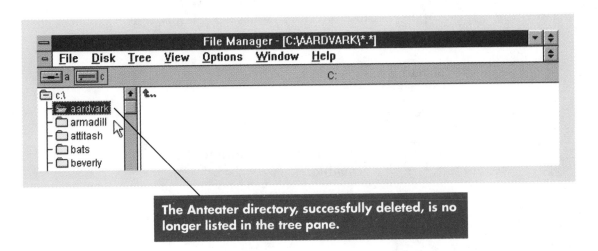

The Anteater directory, successfully deleted, is no
longer listed in the tree pane.

If Anteater had contained files, you would have seen another confirmation dialog box for each file that would be deleted. If that happens to you in the future, you can click on each one individually, or click on Yes to All to bypass confirming each one. This erases the directory and all the files with no further ado.

> **• Note** You can change the settings that cause Windows to display confirmation dialog boxes. You'd do this from the Options menu's Confirmation option, but I suggest that you leave them all on. Even if it slows things down just a little to respond to the boxes, one accidental deletion of an important directory might cost you much more time than a lifetime of confirmations.

## Changing a Directory's Name

Occasionally you'll realize that a directory name could be more descriptive or could more accurately reflect its contents. When this happens, you can rename it. When you rename a directory, all its files stay put. Just the directory's name changes. You can practice with Armadill (remember, the *o* was dropped because directory names can be only eight characters long).

**1.** Click on **armadill** to highlight it.

**2.** Open the **File** menu and choose **Rename**.

**3.** Type in the new directory name. To conform to the eight-letter limit, let's type **armadilo**.

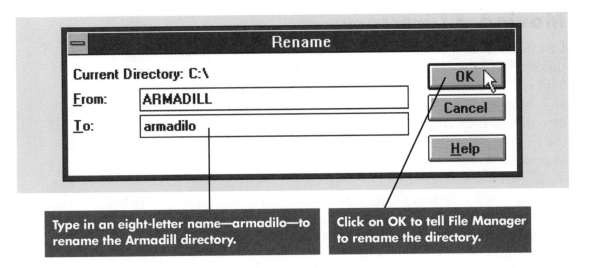

Type in an eight-letter name—armadilo—to rename the Armadill directory.

Click on OK to tell File Manager to rename the directory.

**4.** Click on **OK.** This time Windows doesn't prompt you to confirm because renaming a directory is pretty harmless. The worst thing that could happen is that you decide to change it back.

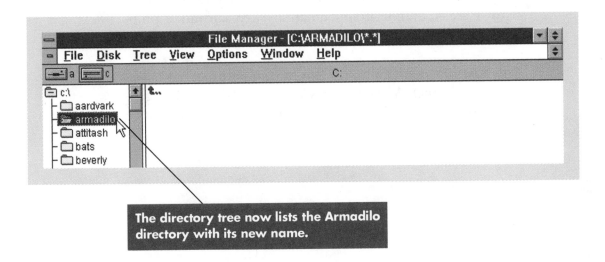

The directory tree now lists the Armadilo directory with its new name.

## Moving a Directory

Last but not least, you can move directories all over the place without much effort or consequence. You may decide that a directory contains a lot of documents that pertain to information in another directory and that you want to combine them. Or perhaps you just created a subdirectory in the wrong directory and you want to move it. Whatever the reason, moving directories is done by dragging them to their new location.

Let's say you decide that the new directories you created above really belong in a directory about wildlife in a certain area of Texas. First we'll create a directory for that area. Then we'll move the other two directories into it.

1. Create a new directory as you did above, naming it **amarillo** this time.

2. Now position the mouse pointer on **aardvark**, then press the button and hold it down as you drag aardvark to amarillo. You'll see an outline around amarillo when aardvark is properly positioned for release.

3. Release the mouse button. (This moving technique is called *drag and drop*.) A dialog box will appear and File Manager will ask you to confirm your request to move the directory.

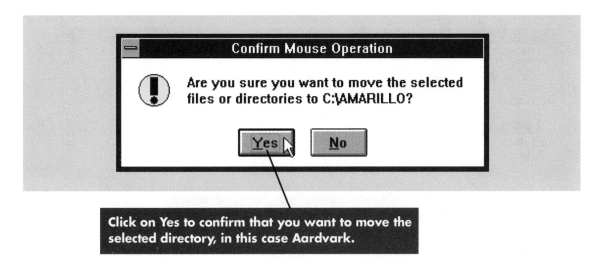

Click on Yes to confirm that you want to move the selected directory, in this case Aardvark.

**4.** Click on **Yes.** You will soon see that aardvark has been moved to amarillo.

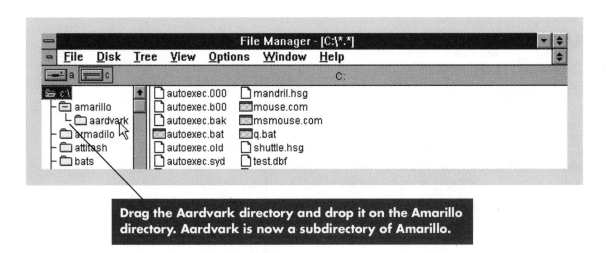

Drag the Aardvark directory and drop it on the Amarillo directory. Aardvark is now a subdirectory of Amarillo.

**5.** Move the armadilo directory in exactly the same way as you just moved aardvark.

You can see that both the Armadilo and Aardvark directories are now in the Amarillo directory. They are subdirectories, as indicated by the fact that they branch off Amarillo rather than off C:.

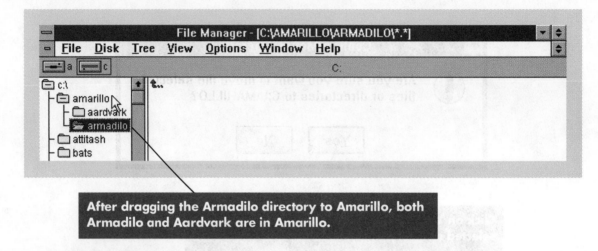

After dragging the Armadilo directory to Amarillo, both
Armadilo and Aardvark are in Amarillo.

Keep in mind that when you move a directory, everything in that directory moves, too. This means that if it has subdirectories, they go along to the new location.

## Viewing Distant Directories Simultaneously

The directories you moved in the last section were all clustered together at the top of the tree because they started with the letter *A*.

But sometimes you have to work with directories at opposite ends of the tree, and they don't both show in the display window even with File Manager maximized. For that you'll need to know how to open two directory windows at once so you can focus on different branches of the tree. It's easy, so let's do it.

You already have one directory window open, so we're halfway there. We just need to open another one.

**1.** Move the mouse pointer to the drive selectors, position it over the **C:** icon, and double-click. The screen looks pretty much the same, but look at the title bar—there's a *2:* after the directory name. That means this is the second window open for the C:\ directory.

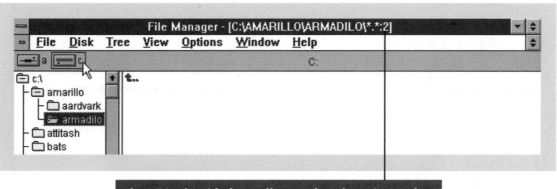

The :2 in the title bar tells you that there is another directory window open, behind this one.

**2.** Open the **Window** menu and choose **Tile**. Presto. You have two identical directory windows, one above the other. You know the top one is active because its title bar is highlighted.

**You know this window is active because its title bar is highlighted.**

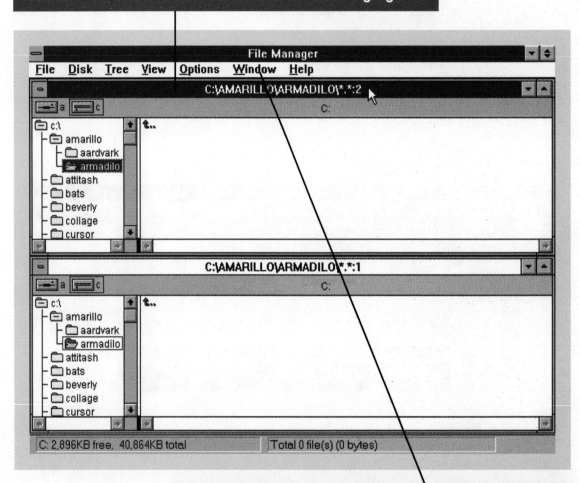

**Choose Tile from the Window menu and the two open windows will arrange themselves one above the other.**

3. Move the pane's border to the right a little in both windows. We're going to expand some branches and we want to make room for the directory names.

4. In the bottom window, highlight the root directory **C:** and create a new directory called *zoo*. Refer to the section at the beginning of this lesson if you don't remember how.

5. Scroll to the bottom of the tree pane to see the new directory in the tree.

With both windows open, let's copy a subdirectory from one directory to another. We'll put the Armadilo directory into the Zoo directory.

6. Drag **armadilo** from its position in the top window to **zoo** in the bottom window. When zoo is outlined, drop armadilo. Again you'll see a confirmation box.

7. Click on **Yes** to confirm the move.

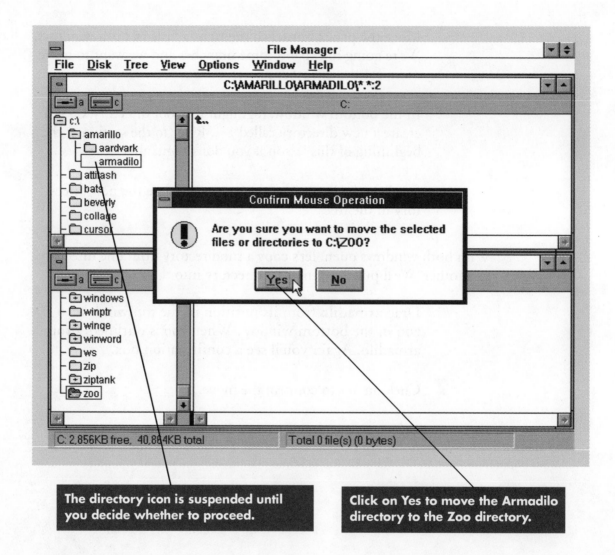

The directory icon is suspended until you decide whether to proceed.

Click on Yes to move the Armadilo directory to the Zoo directory.

Viewing both directory windows satisfies you that the move was successful. The Armadilo subdirectory is now in Zoo, and Aardvark is alone in Amarillo.

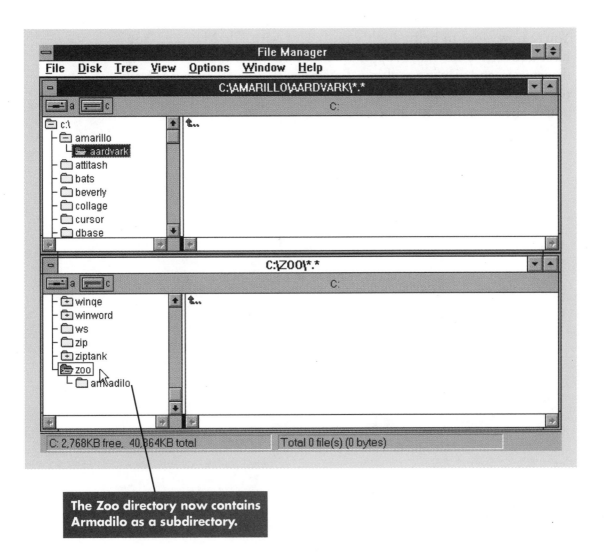

The Zoo directory now contains Armadilo as a subdirectory.

You can have as many directory windows as you want open at once. To arrange all the windows neatly, double-click on the drive icon and choose Tile. When you want to activate one of the windows, just click anywhere within it.

You're now close to being highly proficient with File Manager. You have added to your skills copying, renaming, deleting, and moving directories, and viewing multiple directories at once. Now you're ready to move, copy, rename, and delete files—that will be a lot like what you've already done with directories.

# Working with Files

Everything you've learned in Part Three has been to prepare you for File Manager's main purpose in life—to manage your files. As mentioned earlier, files are the documents you create when working on your computer. Directories and subdirectories are places to keep your documents once you've prepared them.

The scariest part about reorganizing and copying files in DOS is that you can't see what happens after you tell the computer what you want it to do. But not so with File Manager.

When you juggle your files around in File Manager, everything is much more intuitive—you drag things around graphically, so you really get to see where things are going. And, as you saw when we worked with directories in the last lesson, you get at least one chance to change your mind, sometimes two or three (depending on what you're asking File Manager to do). The bigger the potential disaster if you go ahead, the more chances you get to cancel the whole thing.

We'll make copies of the files we work with in this lesson, so you don't have to worry about anything happening to your files. You'll move files between directories and drives, rename them as you go, and finally delete the sample files so they don't cause confusion in the future.

Let's see File Manager in action.

# Copying and Moving Files

Copying files is often done to make back-up copies in case anything happens to your computer or a floppy disk gets damaged. If you have more than one copy of your work you can always load the backup and continue work.

Copying also comes in handy when you want to create a new document that's similar to one you already have. Say you're answering "personals" ads. You want to send each person a basic biography but want to customize the rest of the letter to address each ad's particulars. Write one letter, copy it fifty times, then fill in around the biography—you get the general idea.

Moving files allows you to reorganize your directory for various reasons. Say you used a friend's computer to write your term paper but don't want to leave it there for your friend to use next semester. You would move the file to a floppy disk for safekeeping. Or suppose you wrote a letter to Aunt Martha when you were working on your company's budgets and you accidentally saved the letter in the wrong directory. Just move it from Acme's Budget directory to your Letters directory. With a little practice you shouldn't have any problem.

## Copying Files

Since the Windows directory is one that we all have in common, let's use it as our source of files to copy.

If your screen is still set up as it was at the end of the last lesson, you should see two directory windows.

1. Leave the top window with the root directory displayed at the top of the directory tree pane.

**2.** In the bottom window, scroll the directory tree pane up a little so that the **windows** directory shows if it doesn't already.

**3.** Click on **windows** so its files appear in the contents pane.

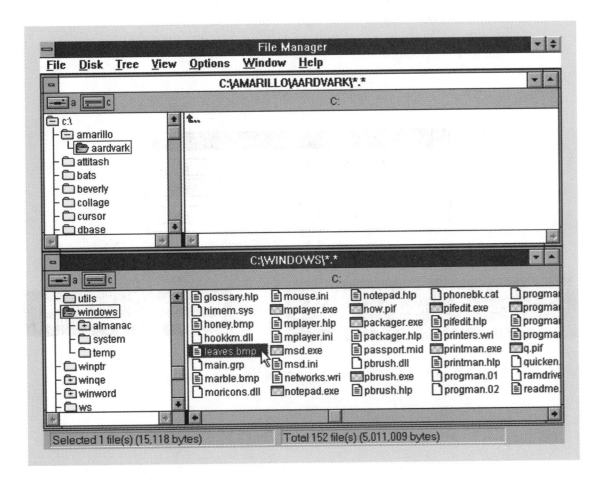

**4.** Using the scroll bar along the bottom of the contents pane, scroll the file listing to the right until you see the file called **leaves.bmp**. (A file with the letters *bmp* after its name is a *bitmapped* picture file.)

**5.** Click on **leaves.bmp** so that it's highlighted.

**6.** Open the **File** menu and choose **Copy**.

**7.** In the dialog box that appears, type **leaves2.bmp** as the new file name. Since we're not going to store the copy somewhere else for now, it has to have a different name than the file we're copying.

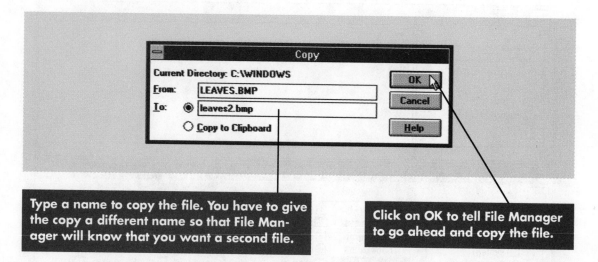

Type a name to copy the file. You have to give the copy a different name so that File Manager will know that you want a second file.

Click on OK to tell File Manager to go ahead and copy the file.

**8.** Click on **OK.** The contents pane now lists the new file copy.

**9.** Click on **leaves2.bmp** to highlight it.

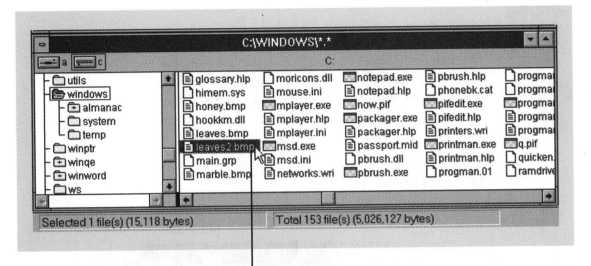

The Windows directory now contains a second copy of LEAVES2.BMP.

Now we'll copy LEAVES2.BMP but this time we'll put the copy in a different directory. We'll copy it a different way, too, using the drag-and-drop technique.

**10.** Press Ctrl (it's somewhere around Shift) and hold it down.

**11.** Still holding Ctrl down, click on **leaves2.bmp** and drag it over to the **zoo** directory.

**12.** When zoo is outlined so you know the file is positioned correctly, "drop" the file (release the mouse button, then release Ctrl).

*Quick Easy*

> **● Note**  When you see a little plus inside the icon of a file you're dragging, it means, "This is an additional copy of the file." If the little icon doesn't have a plus sign in it, you're *moving* the file rather than copying it. You can press **Ctrl** anytime before you release the mouse button to add the plus sign. Likewise, you can release **Ctrl** anytime to remove the plus sign. Play with it to see how readily it turns the plus sign on and off.

**13.** Click on **Yes** in the dialog box.

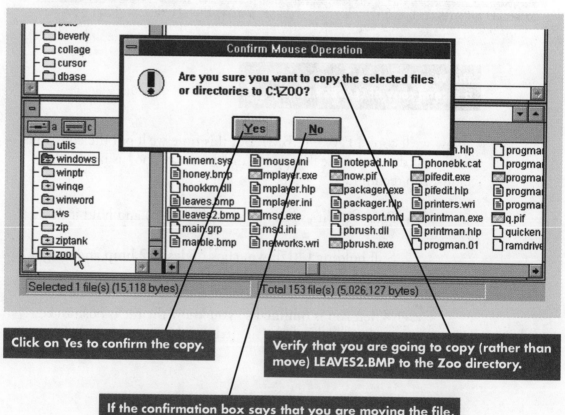

Click on Yes to confirm the copy.

Verify that you are going to copy (rather than move) LEAVES2.BMP to the Zoo directory.

If the confirmation box says that you are moving the file, click on No and start again, this time taking care not to release **Ctrl** until after you release the mouse button.

**14.** Click on **zoo** to list its files in the contents pane. If you copied it correctly, it should be there.

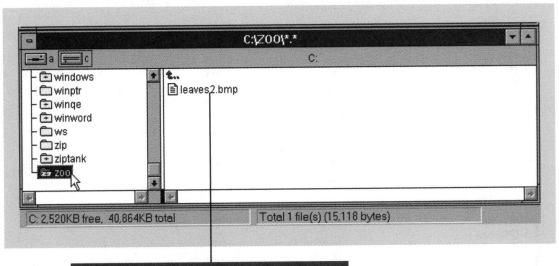

| C:\ZOO\*.* |
| a  c | C: |

- 📁 windows
- 📁 winptr
- 📁 winqe
- 📁 winword
- 📁 ws
- 📁 zip
- 📁 ziptank
- 📂 zoo

🢁 ..
📄 leaves2.bmp

C: 2,520KB free, 40,864KB total | Total 1 file(s) (15,118 bytes)

**LEAVES2.BMP is now in the Zoo directory.**

If you want to make sure that you really copied it from the Windows directory and didn't just move it, take a look by comparing the two directory windows.

**15.** In the top window, scroll to the end of the directory tree until you see the windows directory (you can also go to the end by pressing **End**).

**16.** Click on **windows** to see its contents.

**17.** Scroll to **leaves2.bmp**. If it's there, then you copied it correctly. If it's not, try again.

*Quick&Easy*

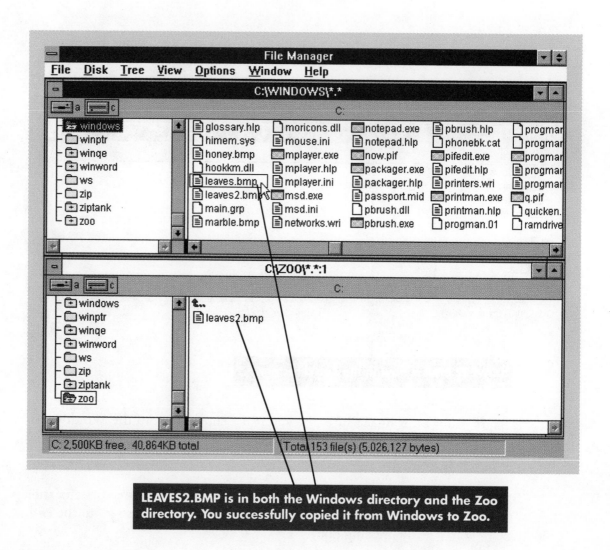

LEAVES2.BMP is in both the Windows directory and the Zoo directory. You successfully copied it from Windows to Zoo.

## Moving Files

Moving files is done much the same as copying, with just a few slight variations. We'll move LEAVES2.BMP from the Windows directory to the Armadilo subdirectory in Zoo.

**1.** Adjust one of your directory windows so that both directories (windows and zoo) show in the tree pane.

**2.** Double-click on the **zoo** directory to expand it if it isn't already.

**3.** Click on **leaves2.bmp** in the contents pane of the **windows** directory, drag it to **armadilo**, the subdirectory below **zoo** in the tree pane, and drop it. (Remember that the outline around armadilo—the destination directory—tells you the file will land there when you drop it.)

**To verify that File Manager will move the file you selected to the Armadilo subdirectory, read the confirmation message.**

File Manager

| File | Disk | Tree | View | Options | Window | Help |

C:\WINDOWS\*.*

windows
winptr
winqe
winword
ws
zip
ziptank
zoo
armadilo

| glossary.hlp | moricons.dll | notepad.exe | pbrush.hlp | progman |
| himem.sys | mouse.ini | notepad.hlp | phonebk.cat | progman |
| honey.bmp | mplayer.exe | now.pif | pifedit.exe | progman |
| hookkm.dll | mplayer.hlp | packager.exe | pifedit.hlp | progman |
| leaves.bmp | mplayer.ini | packager.hlp | printers.wri | progman |

**Confirm Mouse Operation**

⚠ **Are you sure you want to move the selected files or directories to C:\ZOO\ARMADILO?**

[ **Yes** ]  [ **No** ]

windows
winptr
leaves2.bmp

**Click on Yes if the message is correct.**

**Click on No if you need to start again.**

4. After you answer **Yes** to the dialog box, leaves2.bmp is gone from the windows directory and shows up in armadilo.

5. Click on **armadilo** to update the contents pane to display the file.

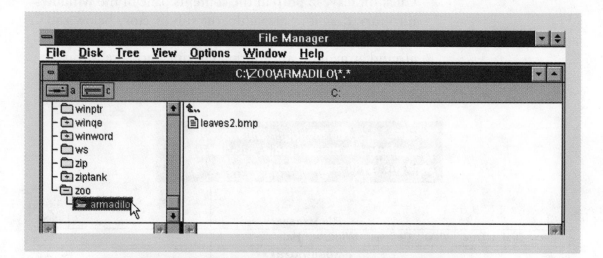

**LEAVES2.BMP is gone from the Windows directory contents pane and is now in the Armadilo subdirectory of the Zoo directory.**

That's all there is to moving files. Now we'll copy and move a few files between the C: and A: since that's what you'll probably do most often.

## Copying and Moving Files between Drives

Now that you know how to copy and move files and to open more than one window so you can work with distant directories, you're going to copy and move files from one drive to another. You'll use this most often to copy or move a file from your computer to a floppy disk, or the reverse.

**1.** Put a floppy disk into your computer.

**2.** In one of the directory windows on your screen, click on the drive selector for that drive to change the window's contents from C: to the floppy. (I'll refer to the floppy drive as A: from here on.)

**3.** Go back to the **C:** directory window. Make sure the **armadilo** subdirectory of **zoo** is still highlighted so you see **leaves2.bmp** in the contents pane.

**4.** Click on **leaves2.bmp** and drag it to the **A:** drive selector of the **C:** directory window. Look at the next picture to see what I mean.

163

*Quick&Easy*

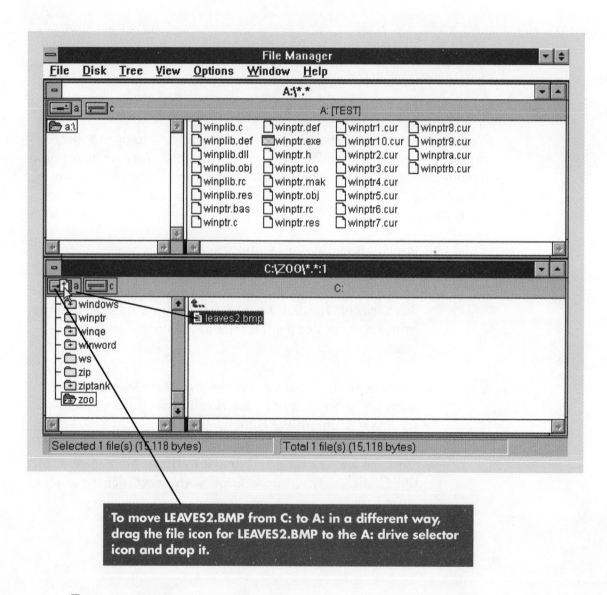

To move LEAVES2.BMP from C: to A: in a different way,
drag the file icon for LEAVES2.BMP to the A: drive selector
icon and drop it.

**5.** Drop the file icon on the drive selector icon and answer **Yes**
to the dialog box.

You just copied LEAVES2.BMP to your floppy disk. Look at the A: directory window to be sure it worked.

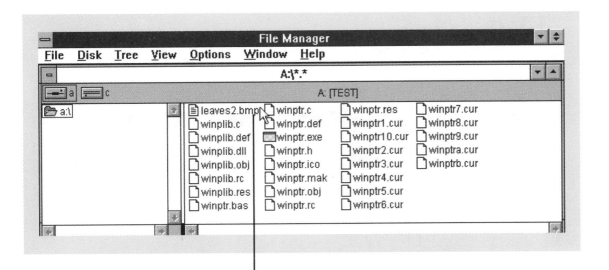

**LEAVES2.BMP now appears in the A: directory window and the C: directory window. You successfully copied it by dropping it on the A: drive icon.**

That's the easiest way to copy from one drive to another, but its limitation is that the file goes into the root directory. If you want to put it in a specific directory, you copy it more like we did in the last section.

**6.** So that we have a new directory to work with, make the A: directory window active and create a directory called *learning.*

**7.** Now go back to the C: window's contents pane and drag **leaves2.bmp** to the A: window's tree pane.

**8.** When the file icon is properly positioned over **learning** (which should be outlined), drop it.

**9.** Click on **Yes** to confirm that you want to copy leaves2.bmp.

*Quick Easy*

**10.** Click on **learning** and leaves2.bmp shows up in the contents pane of the A: window.

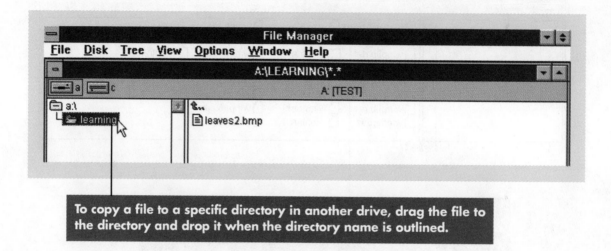

To copy a file to a specific directory in another drive, drag the file to the directory and drop it when the directory name is outlined.

The technique for *moving* files between drives is almost identical to copying, with only one difference.

**1.** In the **C:** directory window, move up to the **amarillo** directory (since our other practice directories have leaves2.bmp files already.)

**2.** Go down to the **A:** directory window. Locate either **leaves2.bmp** file (either the one in the root directory, or the one in learning), and click to highlight it.

**3.** Press **Shift**, then click on **leaves2.bmp** and drag it up to the **C:** window.

**4.** When it's over **amarillo**, release the mouse button, then release **Shift**.

**5.** After answering **Yes** to confirm the move, you'll see that you successfully dropped leaves2.bmp on amarillo. The contents panes reflect the move.

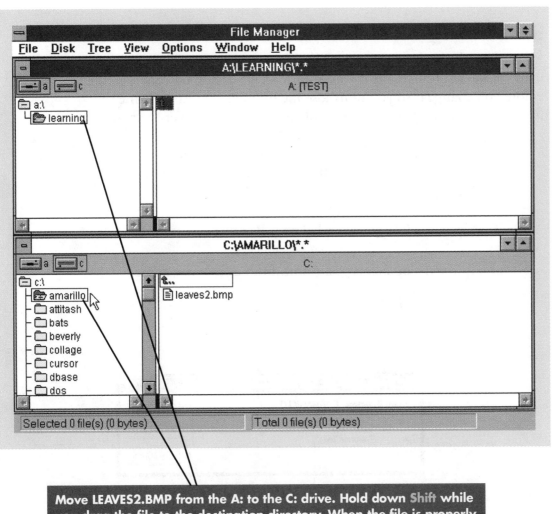

Move **LEAVES2.BMP** from the A: to the C: drive. Hold down Shift while you drag the file to the destination directory. When the file is properly positioned, release the mouse button before releasing Shift.

*Quick&Easy*

That's all there is to moving and copying files between drives and directories. Now you'll rename a file, and then we'll delete the extra copies we made.

## Renaming Files

It's useful to know how to rename files. You may want to make the name more descriptive. Or if you want to make a back-up copy of a file before you change it so you don't lose the original, you can rename the first one before you begin. It's a simple procedure, whatever the reason.

**1.** Since we're already in amarillo, let's rename the leaves2.bmp file there. Click on the file name in the contents pane to highlight it.

**2.** Open the **File** menu and choose **Rename**.

**3.** In the dialog box type **autumn.bmp** as the new name.

**4.** Click on **OK**.

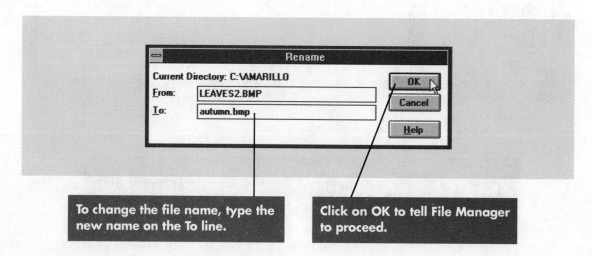

To change the file name, type the new name on the To line.

Click on OK to tell File Manager to proceed.

When you look at the contents pane, you now see AUTUMN.BMP where LEAVES.BMP used to be.

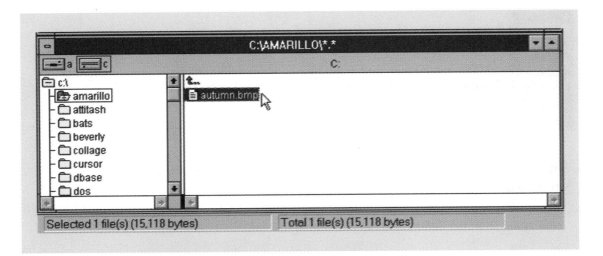

**Autumn.bmp is now in the Amarillo directory. The rename was successful.**

## Deleting Files

The reasons for deleting files are numerous, ranging from eliminating files when they're out of date, to making room on your computer because you have to save something that's more important. When working with real files, delete with some forethought and considerable attention during the operation, just to be sure you don't accidentally erase the wrong files. File Manager's confirmation settings will give you a couple of chances to change your mind, or confirm that you've selected the right files, but it's easy to get into the habit of clicking right through those steps. Deleting files isn't something to do when you're tired or distracted (something I can, unfortunately, say from experience). Do read the confirmation boxes just to make sure the file names displayed are the ones you mean to delete. Then proceed.

**● Note** If you do erase a file accidentally and really need it back, there's some hope, but only if you don't do *anything* else first. File recovery programs such as Norton Unerase, Norton Desktop for Windows, or the unerase program that comes with DOS 5 can unerase deleted files if used before you write any other files to the hard disk.

With that said, let's proceed by deleting AUTUMN.BMP from the Amarillo directory.

**1.** Click on **autumn.bmp** to highlight it if it isn't already.

**2.** Press Del.

**3.** Read the Delete dialog box. It tells you the directory and file name of the file you have told File Manager to delete. Make sure this is correct, then click on **OK**.

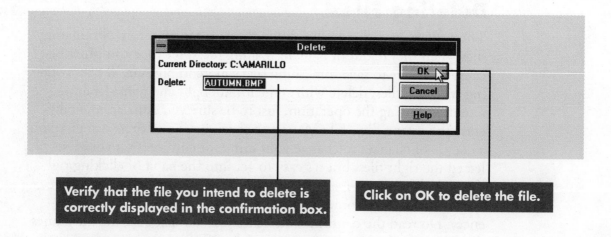

Verify that the file you intend to delete is correctly displayed in the confirmation box.

Click on OK to delete the file.

**4.** Read the Confirm File Delete dialog box. Verify again that the directory and file name are correct, and click on Yes.

Verify again that the correct file is going to be deleted.

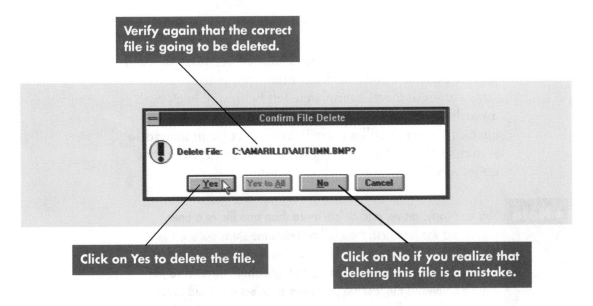

Click on Yes to delete the file.

Click on No if you realize that deleting this file is a mistake.

**5.** Look at the contents pane for **amarillo**. Autumn.bmp is gone from amarillo.

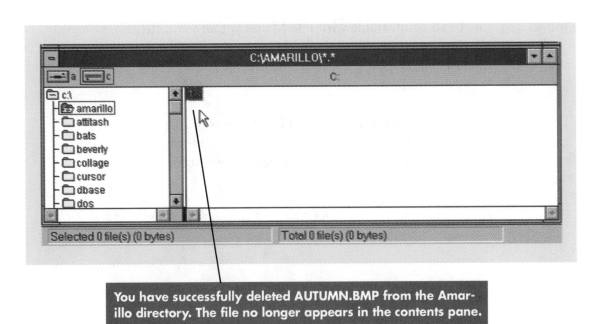

You have successfully deleted AUTUMN.BMP from the Amarillo directory. The file no longer appears in the contents pane.

Let's delete the other file we copied to various places during this lesson.

6. Click on the various directories and subdirectories we used for the exercises. Look in the contents panes to see if any stray copies of leaves2.bmp were left behind. Check both **amarillo** and **aardvark**, then go down to **windows** and check it. There's still a copy in **zoo** and one in **armadilo**, so delete those. Now go to the **A:** window. Delete that copy, too.

> **● Note** You can copy, move, and delete more than one file at a time, too. Select the files first, then follow the same steps outlined in this section. To select several files that are listed together in the contents pane: click on the first file to highlight it, then move the mouse pointer to the last file you want to select and hold down **Shift** while you click again. All the files are selected. To select several files that are not listed together, hold down **Ctrl** while you click on each file name.

You should now be so comfortable with File Manager that you actually consider using it at some time in the future. It's a great tool to have at your disposal, and you'll be glad you put in the time to learn it. (I'm speaking from experience.)

The final three lessons of this section cover a few features of File Manager that can speed up your work in Windows. In the next lesson you'll learn how to search for files when you can't remember where you put them or exactly what you named them.

# Searching for Specific Files

I t's common to create a document, save it when you're finished, then later forget where you put it. You could look in each directory and subdirectory to see if a file is listed, but this can be time consuming, especially as hard drives hold more and more files.

File Manager will search your entire computer or floppy disk for a file and display the results of its search. If you know the name of the file that you're searching for, it's a simple matter of typing it in a dialog box and letting File Manager do the rest. If you know a part of the file name, you can use *wildcards*, standard symbols that represent either a single unknown character (a question mark is used in that case) or a group of unknown characters (an asterisk is used).

First you'll do a file name search, then I'll briefly discuss wildcards.

## Searching for Files by Name

Follow these steps to search for a file by name:

**1.** Open File Manager's **File** menu and choose **Search**.

*Quick Easy*

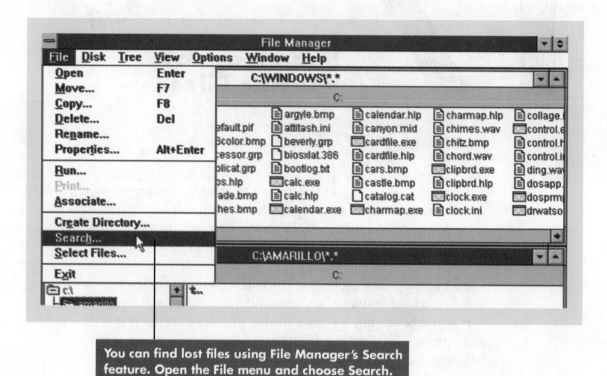

You can find lost files using File Manager's Search feature. Open the File menu and choose Search.

**2.** In the Search dialog box, type **arches.bmp** on the **Search For** line.

● **Note** When using Search, it's important to type in the entire file name, including the three-letter extension after the name.

**3.** Make sure the **Start From** line only says **C:\**. This ensures that File Manager will search the entire drive and not just a few directories.

● **Note** If you press *Home* while the cursor is in the tree pane before you start Search, the Start From line will already say *C:\*.

**4.** Make sure there's an **X** in the **Search All Subdirectories** box.

Enter the complete name, including the extension, of the file you want to find.

Click on OK when the search is set up as you like it.

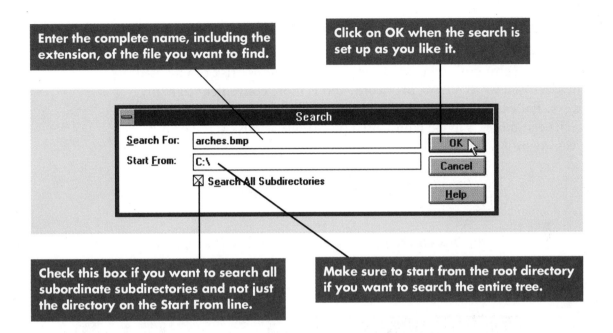

Check this box if you want to search all subordinate subdirectories and not just the directory on the Start From line.

Make sure to start from the root directory if you want to search the entire tree.

**5.** Click on **OK**. It takes a few seconds. If the search was successful, File Manager will display the **Search Results** window.

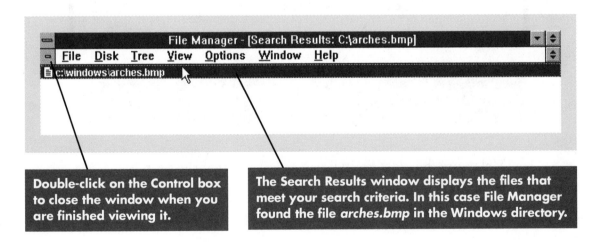

Double-click on the Control box to close the window when you are finished viewing it.

The Search Results window displays the files that meet your search criteria. In this case File Manager found the file *arches.bmp* in the Windows directory.

**6.** Double-click on the **Search Results** window's Control box to close the window when you're finished viewing it.

*Quick & Easy*

## Searching for Files Using Wildcard Symbols

Wildcard symbols are used in place of either a single unknown character (?) or a group of unknown characters (*). The asterisk can be used in place of a word or part of a word, and is more convenient in many cases. For example, a string of question marks representing four letters (????) can more easily be represented by a single asterisk (*). For this reason, we'll talk more about the asterisk.

**1.** Open the **File** menu and choose **Search** to open the Search dialog box.

**2.** On the **Search For** line type **ar*.*** to ask File Manager to search for all files beginning with *ar*.

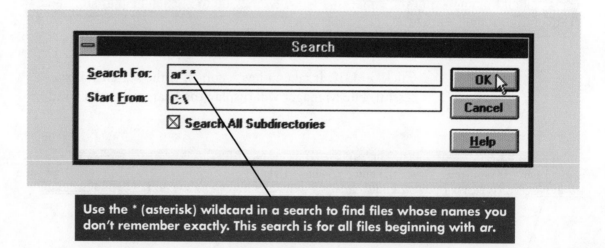

Use the * (asterisk) wildcard in a search to find files whose names you don't remember exactly. This search is for all files beginning with *ar*.

**3.** Make sure the **Start From** line says **C:\** and that the **Search All Subdirectories** box is checked.

**4.** Click on **OK** to see the results of the search.

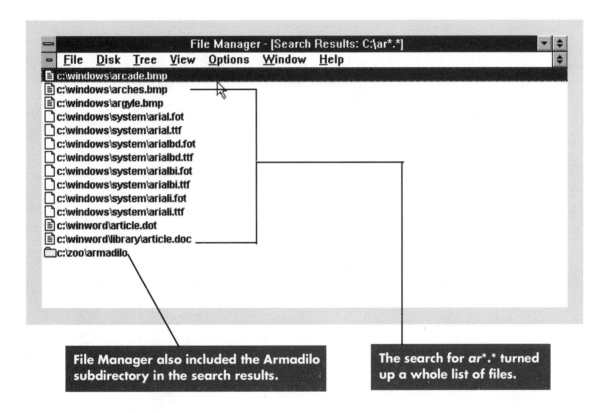

**File Manager also included the Armadilo subdirectory in the search results.**

**The search for *ar\*.\** turned up a whole list of files.**

File Manager found a lot more files than you might have expected. Notice that it also included the Armadilo subdirectory.

You can use * (an asterisk) to replace any part or all of a file name. For example, If you want to look for *all the files* with the *.DOC* extension, you can search for *.DOC, limiting the search quite effectively.

**● Note** The Search Results window works like other File Manager windows. You can select one or more files and move, copy, delete, and rename them, using either the mouse or the File Manager menus as appropriate. You can resize the window and tile it with other directory windows.

It's easy to overlook files that you may have accidentally or purposefully placed in the root directory. If you're not ready to use Search but are at a loss as to the whereabouts of your file, click on the root directory and look at the file listing in the contents pane. Your file could well be there.

Now you are becoming a File Manager master. Next you'll learn how to start programs and run files from File Manager without using the Program Manager windows and icons.

# 18

## Running Programs and Files from File Manager

Although you customarily start an application in Windows by double-clicking on the application's icon (as you learned in Lesson 6), you can also run applications from File Manager. This comes in handy when the program you want to use doesn't have an icon in one of the Program Manager group windows.

Within certain limitations, File Manager also provides an alternative way to open your documents without having to first run the application. It's a lot easier in many cases than going through the sequence to open a file within an application.

## Running a Program from File Manager

Every program has a file in its directory that tells the computer how to set up the screen. Such files have the extension *.EXE*, *.COM*, *.PIF*, or *.BAT* (for *EXEcutable* file, *COMmand* file, *Program Information File*, or *BATch* file). You can double-click on any one of these files in the File

Manager window, and the program will run. You can tell which files
are programs because File Manager gives them a special little icon that
looks like this:

**This icon represents a file that runs
an application's program.**

We're going to run Windows' calculator program from File Manager
using its .EXE file, *CALC.EXE*. Here's how it's done.

**1.** Highlight **windows** in the **C:** drive's tree pane.

**2.** Look in the contents pane and find the **calc.exe** file.

**3.** Double-click on it.

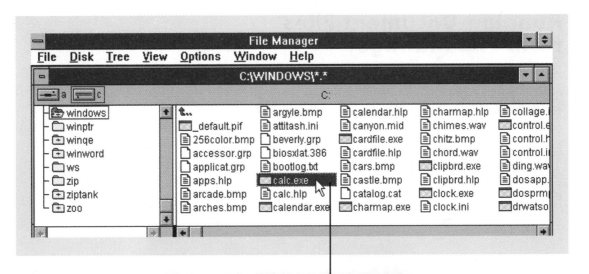

Double-click on the CALC.EXE file name to run the Windows Calculator program.

The Calculator program will come up on the screen. You might remember it from Lesson 6. Don't worry about how to work the Calculator now. The last section of the book covers Windows' accessories, including the Calculator. Close the Calculator window by double-clicking on its Control box.

**• Note** If you're not sure which .EXE file runs a program, keep in mind that you can perform a search for all files with a specific extension (e.g. all the .EXE files) by typing *.EXE in the Search dialog box. The file name usually resembles the application name. For example, the file name for Word for Windows is WINWORD.EXE, and for Windows Write it's WRITE.EXE. When you've located the correct executable file in the Search Results window, double-click on it and the program will run.

## Running Document Files
## from File Manager

When you're doing lots of different things in Windows and you're already in File Manager, it's often easier to run a file from there than it is
to go back to Program Manager. Half the time I forget which group a
program is in anyway, so I use this feature a lot.

This procedure works the same as running an application, but you use
a file instead. There are two kinds of file icons in File Manager. One
looks like a blank little piece of paper, and one looks like a little piece
of paper with writing on it.

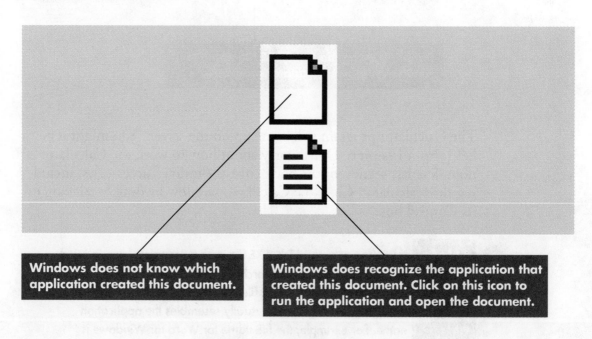

Windows does not know which
application created this document.

Windows does recognize the application that
created this document. Click on this icon to
run the application and open the document.

The file icon with writing on it is one that Windows recognizes. By the
file's three-letter extension, Windows knows what program this file was
created with, whether it was word processing, spreadsheet, graphics, or
something else. For example, if you write a letter to Aunt Martha using
Windows' word-processing program, Write, the file will normally have
the extension .WRI. Windows will recognize this as a file associated
with an application, Write, and will mark it with an icon with writing

on it. (If Windows did not find an extension recognized as one associated with an application, the icon will have no writing on it.) When you double-click on your .WRI file name in File Manager, Windows will run Write first, then open your letter to Aunt Martha. If you had double-clicked on LEAVES2.BMP in Lesson 16, Windows would have run Paintbrush and opened the LEAVES2.BMP file at the same time. Let's try it now.

**1.** Back in the Windows directory listing, scroll over in the contents pane until you see the file **readme.wri**.

**2.** Double-click on it.

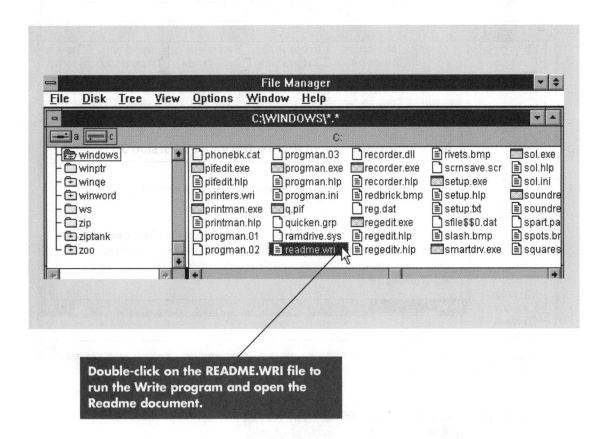

Double-click on the **README.WRI** file to run the Write program and open the Readme document.

**3.** The file will open on your screen. Maximize the window for easier reading. Or close it if you want to go on. Now that you know it's there, you can go back to it in the future, and you may want to read the important Windows information it contains.

> **Click on the Maximize button to see the document on your whole screen.**

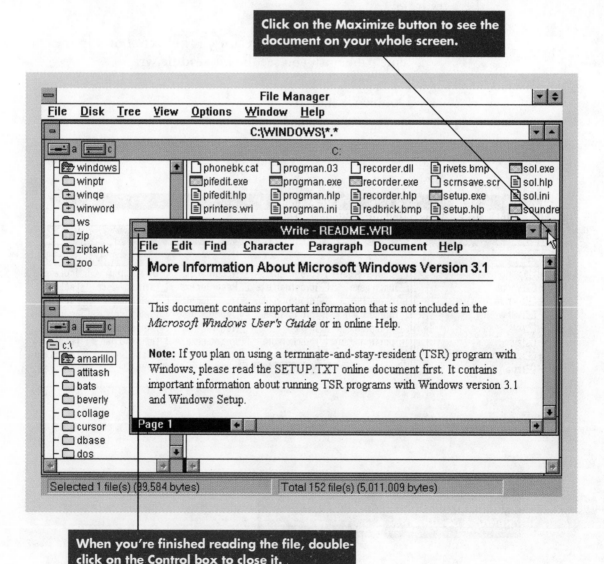

> **When you're finished reading the file, double-click on the Control box to close it.**

**Note** You can make associations for files that don't already have them, but it's a little tricky. If you want to try, consult Help in File Manager using the Associate command on the File menu.

You now know just about all there is to know about managing your files and programs with File Manager. Once you've become comfortable with everything in this section, it'll be easy to explore the more sophisticated aspects of File Manager's operation if the mood should strike you. For most people's uses, what you've learned here is ample.

Now all that's left is a quick look at how to format floppy disks using File Manager. Of course, if you buy formatted disks, you don't need to know this. But when you want to reuse old disks to store new files, it's a good idea to reformat them, because formatting erases them and checks to make sure that the disks are good.

10 MINUTES

# Formatting a Floppy Disk

# 19

Windows' disk formatting function is another that makes your computer so much easier to use that this feature alone could be worth the cost of the program. *If* you format disks, that is. Pre-formatted disks are available (at a premium price) these days, but with Windows all you have to do to format disks is fill in a dialog box.

In case you're in the dark about disk formatting, here's a brief primer. Before your computer can store information on a disk, the disk has to be prepared to receive it. Think of an address book. Before you start writing in names and addresses, you have to make sure there are alphabetical divisions, and lines on each page to keep your writing straight. When you buy a floppy disk, it's usually completely blank. Formatting is the process of adding the necessary *tracks* (section dividers) and *sectors* (lines) so that data can be written onto the disk.

## Sizing Up and Formatting a Floppy Disk

Before you start formatting, it helps to know the size (in storage space) of your floppy disk, although that's not essential. Sometimes the size is printed on the disk. If all you see on the disk label is a code like MFD-1DD, look on the box that the disks came in. The size should be there somewhere. Common sizes for 3-1/2″ floppies are 720K and 1.44MB. 5-1\4″ floppies are commonly 360K and 1.2MB.

If you're using old disks and their size isn't apparent, don't worry. An extra step or two when you format them will solve the problem.

**1.** If **File Manager** isn't open, open it.

**2.** Insert a disk in your floppy drive.

**3.** Open the **Disk** menu and choose **Format Disk**.

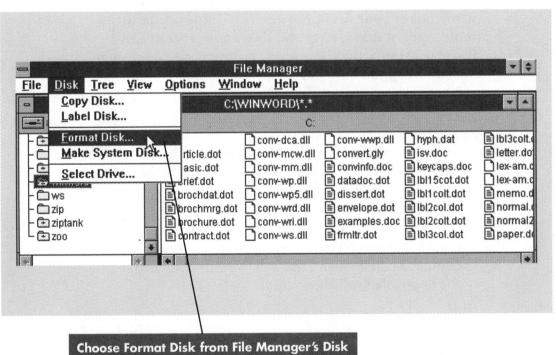

Choose Format Disk from File Manager's Disk menu to open the Format dialog box.

**4.** In the Format Disk dialog box that appears, you have to enter some choices. First make sure that the drive letter correctly indicates which drive the disk is in. If you only have one floppy drive, its letter will already be entered. If you need to change it, click on the arrow to the right of the drive letter to reveal your choices, then click on the correct one.

**● Note** NEVER choose C: as the disk to format. You will erase your computer's entire hard disk—Windows and all. Normally you can only do this from DOS, but be careful, anyway.

**5.** If the disk size already displayed on the **Capacity** line is wrong, open your list of choices by clicking on the arrow to the right of the capacity, and click on the correct size. If you're not sure of the size, start by choosing the higher number (the MB choice is higher than the K). Don't worry about making a mistake, I'll explain later what to do if you choose a number too high.

**6.** If you want to, type a name for the disk in the **Label** space. Later, when you look at the disk in File Manager, this name will appear on the drive selector line of the directory window.

**7.** It's not very likely that you'll want to do this often, but if you want to boot up your computer from the floppy, choose the option **Make System Disk** and Windows will add files to the floppy that will allow this.

**8.** If you want to erase all the disk's files and use it again, click on **QuickFormat**. It's much faster than formatting the normal way, or erasing the files one by one. However, it doesn't erase every bit of your data. Someone could recover part or all of it using an unerase program. (Don't use Quick Format if you're formatting a new disk. The first time you format a disk the computer needs to check every sector on the disk to make sure none are damaged.)

**9.** When all the settings are correct, click on **OK**.

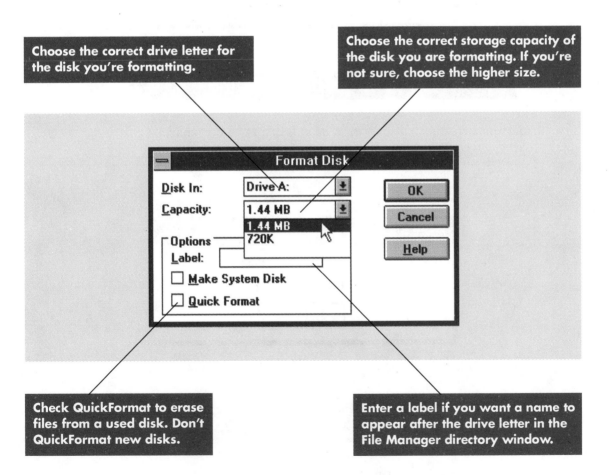

Choose the correct drive letter for the disk you're formatting.

Choose the correct storage capacity of the disk you are formatting. If you're not sure, choose the higher size.

Check QuickFormat to erase files from a used disk. Don't QuickFormat new disks.

Enter a label if you want a name to appear after the drive letter in the File Manager directory window.

**10.** The **Confirm Format Disk** dialog box appears, warning you
that if you proceed, everything on the disk will be erased.
Click on **Yes**.

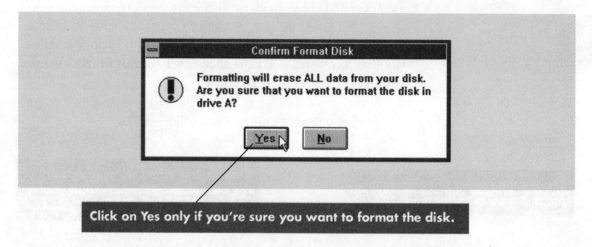

Click on Yes only if you're sure you want to format the disk.

The formatting will begin, and Windows will display a box that
shows you its progress.

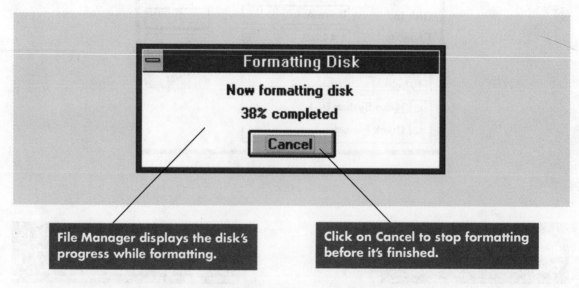

File Manager displays the disk's
progress while formatting.

Click on Cancel to stop formatting
before it's finished.

**11.** When the disk is finished, you'll see the following box.
Unless you want to format another disk now, click on **No**.

When the disk is finished formatting, File Manager tells you how much storage capacity the disk has.

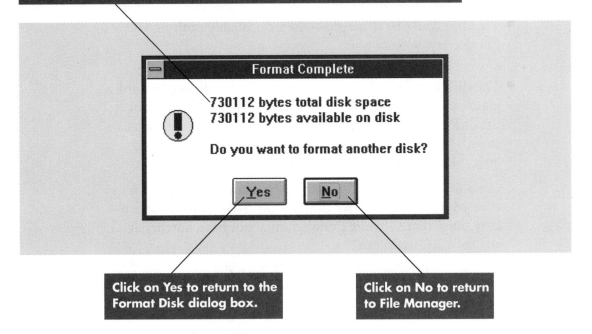

**Format Complete**

730112 bytes total disk space
730112 bytes available on disk

Do you want to format another disk?

Yes     No

Click on Yes to return to the Format Disk dialog box.

Click on No to return to File Manager.

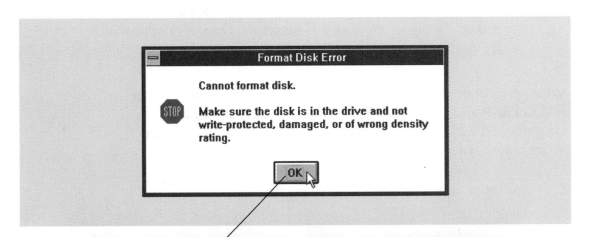

**Format Disk Error**

Cannot format disk.

Make sure the disk is in the drive and not write-protected, damaged, or of wrong density rating.

OK

If this box appears, click on OK to return to the Format Disk dialog box. Either change the storage capacity setting, insert another disk, or check the write-protect tab on the bottom of the disk. Then try again.

If you see a Format Disk Error dialog box like the one in the previous figure, a few things could be wrong:

- The disk could be damaged—there's probably nothing you can do. Try another one.

- The disk may be write-protected. On 3-1/2″ disks (the hard plastic ones) there's a little tab in the corner on the back of the disk that you can open or close. You want the tab to be closed. If there is no tab but something else is blocking the hole (like a piece of tape), remove it.

    On one side of a 5-1/4″ disks there is a cut-out notch. If it's covered with tape, remove that. (Some 5-1/4″ disks, particularly those that software came on, may not have notches at all. You can't use these.)

    In either case, after you have altered the write-protect switch or notch, reinsert the disk and try again.

- You may have chosen the wrong size (storage capacity) for the disk. If you weren't sure what size your disk was and picked the higher number, as I suggested, chances are this is the problem. Try again with the lower number.

Although right now it may seem like a lot to remember, when you get used to File Manager you can easily juggle your files and directories, and you can double- and triple-check everything easily. No disasters. No irritation. No more lost files.

Congratulations. You're an accomplished file manager.

# PART FOUR

# Windows Accessories

**H**ere, in the last part of the book, I'll talk about a few of the accessory programs that you get with Windows, and you'll get to experiment with them a bit. Though they aren't the most powerful programs, these freebies aren't bad, and the price is right. Several of them—notably Write, Notepad, and Paintbrush—I use a lot. You've already played with the Calculator, so I won't cover that here. Calendar and Cardfile are useful for organizing your time and your notes, so I'll guide you through those, too. The remaining accessories—Terminal, Clock, Recorder, Character Map, Media Player, Sound Recorder, and Object Packager—won't be discussed here. They are either self-explanatory or beyond this book's scope.

10 MINUTES

# Scheduling Appointments with Calendar

# 20

As I mentioned in Part Two, Calendar is a little program for keeping your appointments straight. You can use it to bring up a monthly calendar on the screen rather than nailing one to the wall. It calculates the layout of every month for any year between 1980 and 2099—something my wall calendar isn't up to doing. You can also set Calendar to nudge you with an alarm at any number of predetermined times on specific days.

## Running Calendar

**1.** Find **Calendar** in the **Accessories** group and run it.

The calendar should come up with today's date showing, so yours will be different than this one. The Day view is illustrated in the next picture. This view allows you to enter appointments for the date indicated, make notes about the appointments, and set alarms to remind you to do something.

Use these scroll buttons to move from day to day.

Status line shows the current time and date.

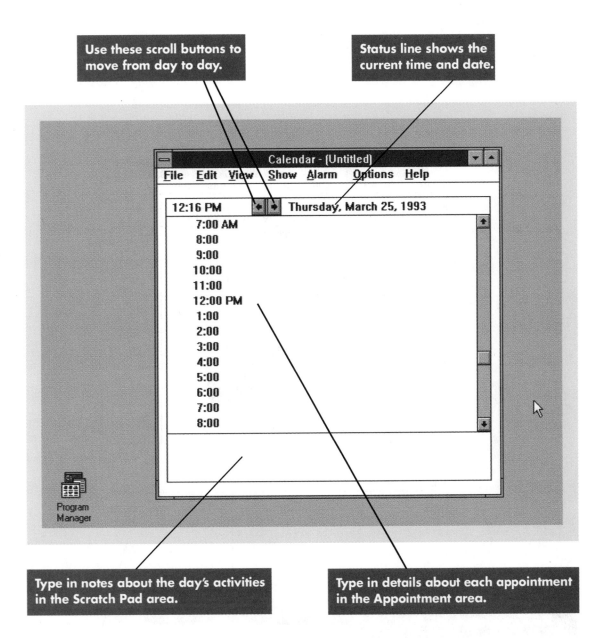

Calendar - [Untitled]

File   Edit   View   Show   Alarm   Options   Help

12:16 PM          Thursday, March 25, 1993

7:00 AM
8:00
9:00
10:00
11:00
12:00 PM
1:00
2:00
3:00
4:00
5:00
6:00
7:00
8:00

Program
Manager

Type in notes about the day's activities in the Scratch Pad area.

Type in details about each appointment in the Appointment area.

*Quick Easy*

**2.** Open the **View** menu and choose **Month** to see the Month view.

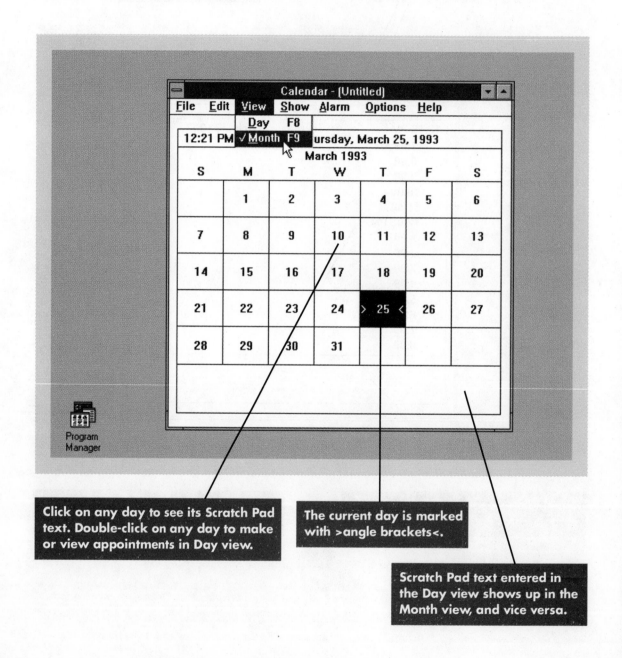

Click on any day to see its Scratch Pad text. Double-click on any day to make or view appointments in Day view.

The current day is marked with >angle brackets<.

Scratch Pad text entered in the Day view shows up in the Month view, and vice versa.

## Jumping to a Specific Date

If you want to jump to a specific date this month, just click on the appropriate square in the Month view. If you want to jump to a distant date—say, several months away—just open the Show menu and choose Date.

> To jump to a specific day of the year, use this command and type the date in the ensuing dialog box.

Then type the desired date into the resulting dialog box and click on OK.

## Entering Appointments

As a default, new calendars will have time increments set to the hour. You may want to use half-hour or quarter-hour intervals. From the Day view, open the Options menu and choose Day Settings to make these changes.

Then, to actually enter an appointment:

1. Click on the time, and the blinking text cursor appears to the right. Begin typing. You can enter up to 80 characters per appointment. If you need more room, you'll have to enter it in the Scratch Pad area.

**2.** To enter a time that's not on the list (such as 3:47), open the
**Options** menu and choose **Special Time**.

**3.** Type the time in the Special Time text box and choose AM
or PM. Click on **Insert** to add the time to the daily calendar.

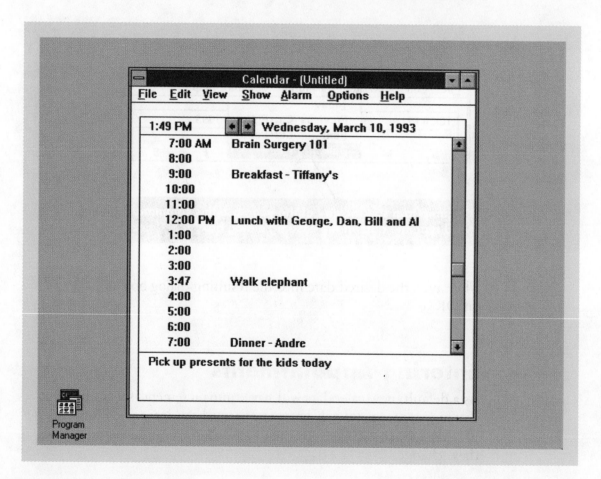

# Setting Alarms

You can set as many alarms to go off during the day as you like.
(Some of us need lots.) Try setting an alarm for the Special Time you
created, 3:47.

**1.** Switch to **Day** view, if you're not already there.

**2.** Select the correct day.

**3.** Position the cursor next to **3:47** by clicking on it.

**4.** Open the **Alarm** menu and choose **Set**. A small bell appears to the left of the alarm time.

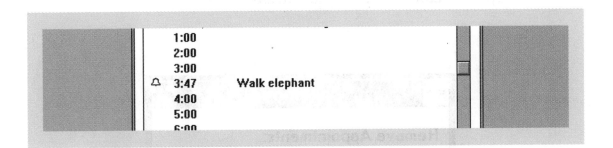

Set an alarm by clicking on the time, opening the Alarm menu, and then choosing Set. Remove the alarm setting by choosing the command again.

**● Note** Alarms won't work unless the Calendar is running, so if you intend to use them, make sure you run Calendar and open the correct calendar file (the one where the alarm is set) when you start up Windows.

When the alarm time comes along, you'll hear four beeps. If the Calendar window is open, you'll see a dialog box announcing the appointment. Click on OK. If Calendar is minimized, its icon will flash on the desktop until you open the window and click on OK in the announcement dialog box.

**● Note** If the Calendar icon or inactive window is covered by another window, you'll have to switch to Calendar from the Task List to OK the dialog box.

## Removing Appointments

From time to time you might want to remove appointments.

**1.** Open the **Edit** menu and choose **Remove**.

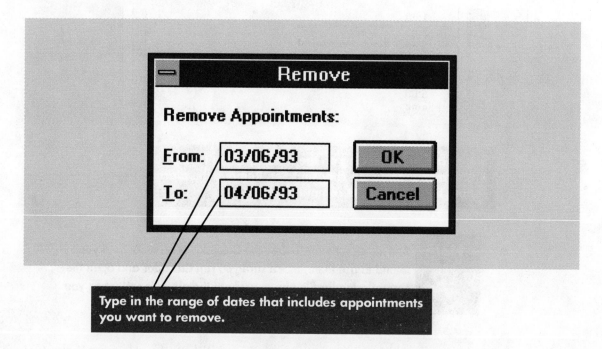

Type in the range of dates that includes appointments you want to remove.

**2.** In the **Remove** dialog box, type in the range of dates that includes appointments you want to remove and click on **OK**.

## Printing Your Appointments

You can print out your appointments on paper to take with you.
Here's how:

**1.** Set up the printer.

**2.** Open the **File** menu and choose **Print**.

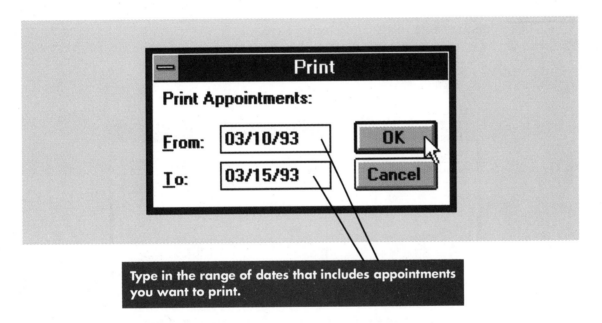

Type in the range of dates that includes appointments
you want to print.

**3.** Fill in the start and end dates, or just click on **OK** for the
current day.

## Saving Your Calendar File

You have to save your appointments in a file, just as you do with any
other type of document. If you don't save your appointments, you'll
lose them.

Additionally, running Calendar when you start Windows won't open your appointment file automatically. It just runs the Calendar program with a blank set of appointments. To bring up your appointments, you have to open your previously saved file via the File menu.

Here are the steps to follow:

**1.** The first time you use Calendar, set up some appointments.

**2.** Open the **File** menu and choose **Save**.

**3.** You'll be greeted by the familiar **Save As** box:

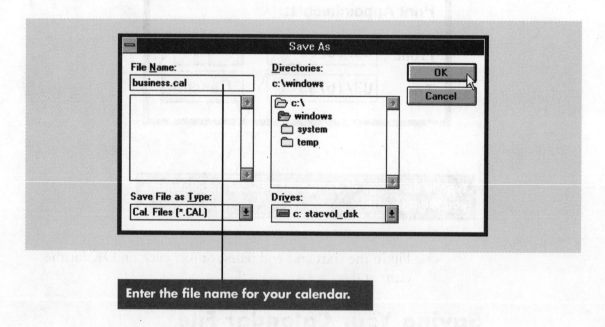

Enter the file name for your calendar.

**4.** Type in a name for the file, choose the directory where you want to save it, and click on **OK**.

Now you've created the basis of your calendar file on disk. The next time you run Calendar, choose Open from the File menu, and choose your calendar file from the dialog box. Your appointments will all be there. If you make changes to the file (by adding, editing, or deleting appointments) you'll be prompted to save the changes when you exit Windows or close Calendar.

After seeing how easy the Calendar is to use, finding your way around Windows should be getting pretty intuitive. In the next few lessons I'll cover the basics of Cardfile for organizing notes; the two word processing programs, Notepad and Write; and finish off with an overview of the versatility of Paintbrush.

# Jotting Down Notes with Notepad

**Y**ou can use Notepad to jot down telephone notes, make a shopping list, or write a memo to an associate. Notepad is a very simple text editor that makes files with no formatting to speak of (such as italic or bold), so Notepad files can be picked up and used by almost any word processing program.

You've already run Notepad earlier in this book. It's as easy as finding the program's icon in the Accessories group and double-clicking. Then you just type away.

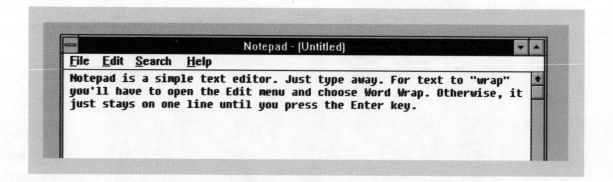

1. Type the text that you see in the picture.

**2.** Note the comment about getting the text to *wrap*. If you don't turn on Word Wrap, the words just keep moving to the right. The screen scrolls, too, unless you press Enter at the end of every line, which is a pain. So I just turn on **Word Wrap** as soon as I run Notepad. This always keeps the text within the constraints of the window. Turn it on now.

**3.** Resize the **Notepad** window smaller and the words will automatically rewrap to the size of the window.

**4.** Resize the **Notepad** window back to its previous larger size.

## Saving and Opening Notepad Files

Just as with any other program, you'll have to save your Notepad files to disk if they're to be found the next time you want to use them. Let's save this file and then open an existing one so we can experiment with some of Notepad's other features.

Since you're getting pretty familiar with saving files by now, I won't take you through all the steps. Just choose Save from Notepad's File menu. You know how to do the rest.

Now let's open a file to play with. It's done the same way you open any file in Windows, using the File Open dialog box.

**1.** From the **File** menu, choose **Open**.

**2.** Open **setup.txt**.

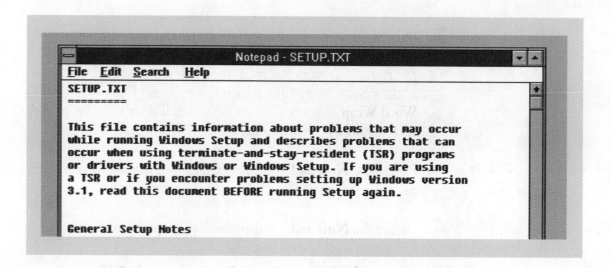

## Navigating in Notepad

There are a couple of keys you can use to quickly navigate within Notepad files. These keys also work with lots of other Windows programs, such as Write.

| KEY | MOVES CURSOR TO |
| --- | --- |
| Home | Start of the line |
| End | End of the line |
| Ctrl-Home | Start of the file |
| Ctrl-End | End of the file |

Try playing with these keys within the SETUP.TXT file.

## Searching for Text

If you can't easily find the section of text you're looking for, use the Find command on the Search menu and Notepad will find it for you.

Say you're wondering if there is anything in the SETUP.TXT file about Stacker, the hard-disk extender program you're using. Try this:

1. Press **Ctrl-Home** to return to the beginning of the file, if necessary.

2. Open the **Search** menu, and choose **Find**.

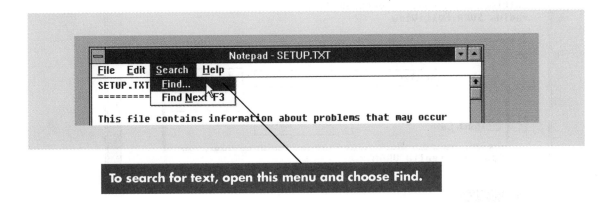

To search for text, open this menu and choose Find.

A dialog box appears, like the one below.

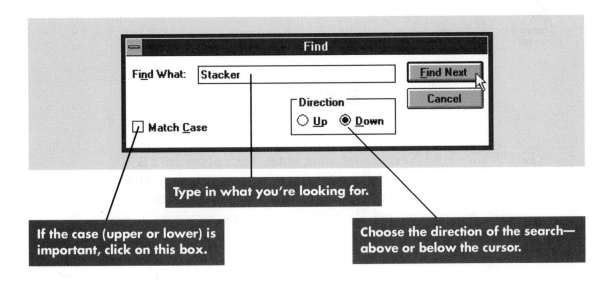

Type in what you're looking for.

If the case (upper or lower) is important, click on this box.

Choose the direction of the search— above or below the cursor.

**2.** Fill in **Stacker** and click on **Find Next**.

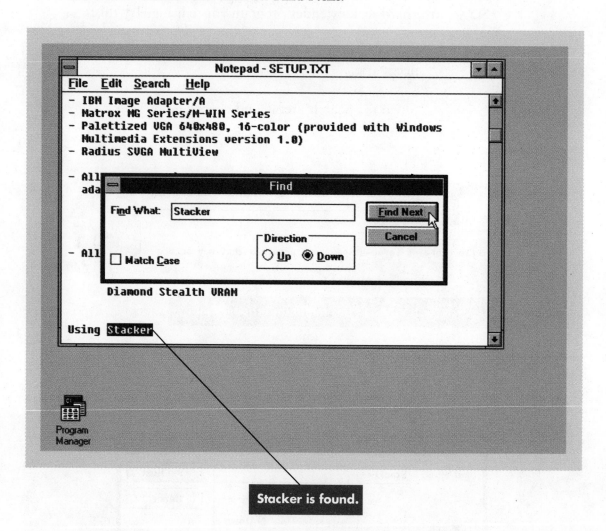

Stacker is found.

**3.** Click on **Find Next** several more times. Each occurrence is found. Or, you can click on **Cancel** to halt the search. If you keep clicking on Find Next, eventually you'll be told that no more occurrences could be found. In that case, you'll see a dialog box like the one in the next figure.

## Closing Notepad Files

That's about all there is to Notepad's most frequently used features. Now all that's left is leaving Notepad. Like saving files, the way to close Notepad should be getting pretty familiar to you by now. Use any of the customary ways:

- Choose Exit from the File menu,

- Choose Close from Notepad's Control menu, or

- Double-click on the Control box.

If you made any changes to SETUP.TXT while experimenting with Notepad, you'll see a dialog box when you close, asking if you want to save the changes. In this case, click on No, and you return to Program Manager.

Most applications will prompt you in this way. If you forget to save before you exit, you aren't likely to lose your work unless you click on No. To save before exiting, when the dialog box asks if you want to save, click on Yes, then fill in the File Save dialog box as usual.

## Some Final Notes about Notepad

Notepad has a lot of features that are common to other application programs. Look through the menus to see available options. You can print from the File menu; delete, move, and copy text from the Edit menu; and, as with all Windows programs, you can get help using Notepad from the Help menu. Using these features will soon be second nature to you.

# Filing Information with Cardfile

Cardfile is one of my favorite accessory programs. I use it all the time to keep track of people's phone numbers, make notes about things I have to do, and store bits of information about pending projects.

Cardfile works like a Rolodex or a box of index cards. Each card has room on it for up to 11 lines of text, and a title line called the *index line.* The index line is used for identification, just so you can quickly see the topic of each card. Cardfile automatically alphabetizes the cards according to the index line.

## Adding New Cards

To get started with Cardfile do this:

1. Run **Cardfile** from Program Manager's **Accessories** group. Up comes an empty card.

*Quick Easy*

**The Status line shows which view you're in and how many cards there are.**

**Scroll arrows can be used to flip through the cards.**

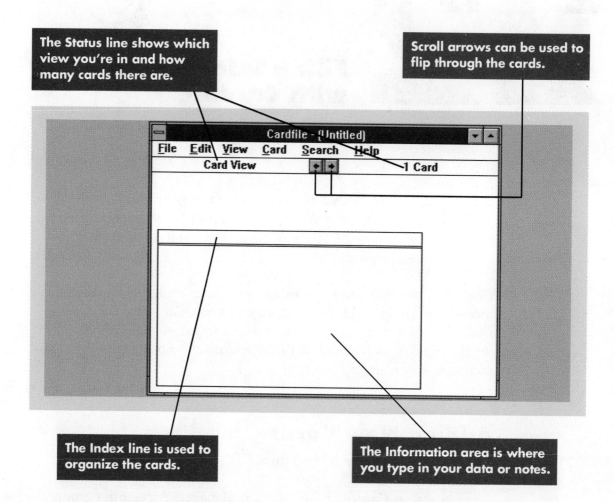

Cardfile - (Untitled)

File   Edit   View   Card   Search   Help

Card View                      1 Card

**The Index line is used to organize the cards.**

**The Information area is where you type in your data or notes.**

**2.** Double-click on the index line so you can input the first card's index information. Up comes a little dialog box:

Index

Index Line:    Becky Thatcher

OK          Cancel

**3.** Type the information you want to appear on the index line, and click on **OK**. The index line is added to the card, and the text cursor drops down into the information area. Type in some relevant material about Becky.

**4.** Open the **Card** menu and choose **Add** (or press **F7**). Enter the index line for your next card, and click **OK**. A new card is added to the front of the stack. Add some information if you like.

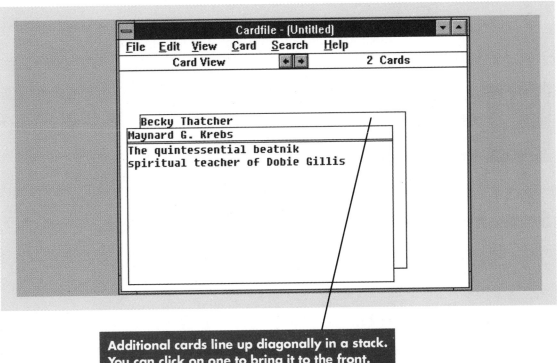

Additional cards line up diagonally in a stack. You can click on one to bring it to the front.

Notice that the status line now reads "2 Cards."

**5.** Click on Becky's card to bring it to the front. Click on the scroll buttons to flip through the cards.

## Editing the Index Line and Information Area

From time to time you may have to edit an index line or the information area. This is easy.

**1.** Scroll to the card you want.

**2.** Double-click on the index line to open the index and edit the index line if you wish.

**3.** Click on **OK**.

**4.** Click in the information area to edit it, using the standard Windows text editing procedures.

 **Note** If you have more related information than will fit on one card, create another one with the same index line and put in a 2 at the end (for example, Venezuela and Venezuela2). This way the cards will always stay together in the stack.

# Searching for Text in a Stack of Cards

Once you have a bunch of cards in the stack, searching for someone's name will become a hassle. There are a couple of ways to deal with this.

## Viewing Cards in a List

The first way is to change the view so that instead of cards, you just see a list of all the index lines.

**1.** Open the **View** menu and choose **List**. The screen now changes to look like this (I've added some additional cards to illustrate the point):

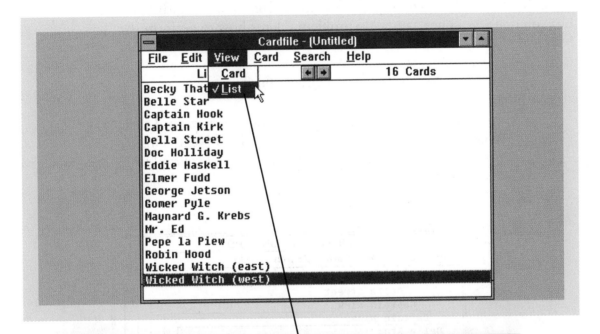

Change the view to List; only the index lines show, but you can see more of them. Highlight one, change to Card, and it's on top of the stack.

**2.** If you click on one of the lines and then choose **Card** from the **View** menu, you'll see the card's information area.

## Searching for Text on a Card

Once you have lots of notes on cards, it's likely that you'll forget where some little gem of information is located. Cardfile can help you.

Suppose you're looking for information about Tom Sawyer's girlfriend, but you don't recall her name. No problem. Here's how to perform the search:

1. Open the **Search** menu and choose **Find**.

2. Type in the information, even if it's only one key word that might be on the card, and then click on **Find Next**. This works just like the Find command in Notepad covered in the last lesson.

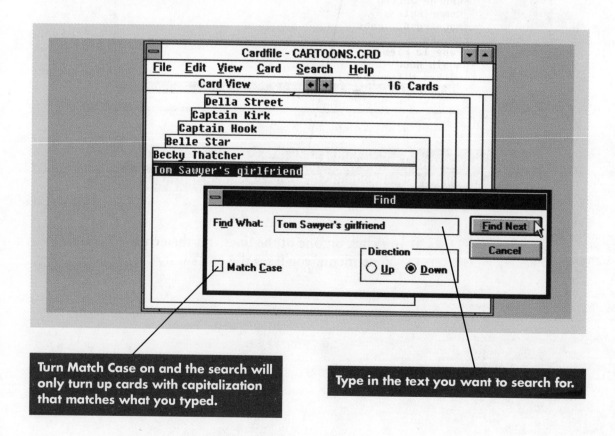

Turn Match Case on and the search will only turn up cards with capitalization that matches what you typed.

Type in the text you want to search for.

**3.** When you get to the card you want, click on **Cancel**. You've found the card you were looking for.

## Deleting Cards

Sometimes you'll want to delete a card because its information is obsolete. Just do this:

**1.** Bring the card to the front of the stack.

**2.** Open the **Card** menu and choose **Delete**.

**3.** Answer **Yes** to the dialog box that asks for confirmation.

**• Note** Be careful when deleting cards. They can't be restored once they're deleted.

## Saving and Reloading Your Work

Once again, don't forget to save your work before you close Cardfile, or it won't be around later when you want it. Use the File menu and the Save command to do this. Cardfile files always have a .CRD extension (for example, PEOPLE.CRD). After saving your file, close Cardfile by one of the usual methods.

Once your card file is saved, you can open it using the Open command on the File menu. Keep in mind that you can have more than one card file open at a time, too. Just run Cardfile more than once from the Program Manager. By the way, you can also run more than one notepad and calendar at a time the same way.

# Simple Word Processing with Write

# 23

One of the most useful freebie programs supplied with Windows is called Windows Write, or just Write. This is a simple word processor. While it doesn't sport the variety of frills seen in high-priced programs like Word for Windows or WordPerfect, it will do for basic tasks like writing letters, reports, or anything that doesn't require fancy formatting. In fact, I use Write pretty frequently just because it's there. It's sort of my everyday word processing workhorse.

Check it out:

1. Run **Write** from the **Accessories** group, as you have with the other programs.

2. Rather than typing in a whole mess of text, let's open a file that already exists. Open the **File** menu and choose **Open**. There are several Write files already on your hard disk, in the **windows** directory. Choose the one called **readme.wri**. (This is the same file we opened by double-clicking on its icon before, but we're opening it in a different way this time.)

3. Imagine Write's window to be approximately as wide as the illustrations below, so the text is easier to work with.

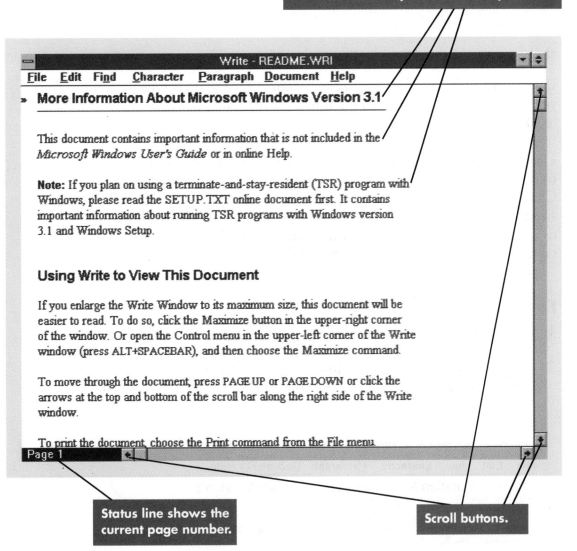

Write can use many different kinds of type, limited only by the number of fonts you have installed on your Windows system.

**Write - README.WRI**

File   Edit   Find   Character   Paragraph   Document   Help

» **More Information About Microsoft Windows Version 3.1**

This document contains important information that is not included in the *Microsoft Windows User's Guide* or in online Help.

**Note:** If you plan on using a terminate-and-stay-resident (TSR) program with Windows, please read the SETUP.TXT online document first. It contains important information about running TSR programs with Windows version 3.1 and Windows Setup.

**Using Write to View This Document**

If you enlarge the Write Window to its maximum size, this document will be easier to read. To do so, click the Maximize button in the upper-right corner of the window. Or open the Control menu in the upper-left corner of the Write window (press ALT+SPACEBAR), and then choose the Maximize command.

To move through the document, press PAGE UP or PAGE DOWN or click the arrows at the top and bottom of the scroll bar along the right side of the Write window.

To print the document, choose the Print command from the File menu.

Page 1

Status line shows the current page number.

Scroll buttons.

219

Once the file loads up, you can see that Write is capable of more varieties of type than is Notepad, where all the letters look the same. Let's play with some of that formatting.

## Formatting Your Text

If you were creating a new document, all you'd have to do is type in your text. In Write, the text wraps automatically; in Notepad, you had to turn on wrapping.

Once you have your text typed in, or even as you enter it, you'll want to start fine-tuning the formatting. There are two types of formatting: Character formatting and Paragraph formatting. You can change the size and typeface of letters, and make them bold, italic, or underlined, using Character formatting. You can center text, and set justification, tabs, and indents, with Paragraph formatting.

### Formatting Characters

To get the hang of character formatting, we'll change a few words.

1. Before you can do any formatting, you have to select some text. Select the word **not** as you see below.

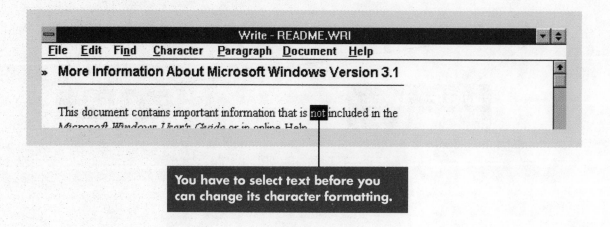

You have to select text before you can change its character formatting.

**2.** Let's make this word bold, for emphasis. Open the **Charac-**
**ter** menu.

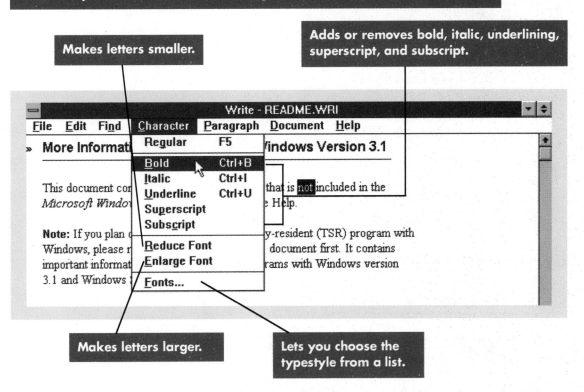

Choose any of these commands to change the formatting of the selected text.

Makes letters smaller.

Adds or removes bold, italic, underlining, superscript, and subscript.

Makes letters larger.

Lets you choose the typestyle from a list.

**3.** Choose **Bold** from the menu. The word *not* changes to bold.

**4.** Try some other settings from the same menu now, such as
Underline or Italic.

**• Note** When you apply a format (like Bold) to a word, selecting the text again and looking at the menu reveals a check mark next to the command. These are "toggle" commands. Each time you select the command you turn it on and off, like a light switch. Selecting Bold again "un-bolds" the letters, and the check mark goes off.

**5.** Let's change the font. Select the whole paragraph. Notice that if you move the cursor to the left margin, the cursor changes to a right-facing arrow. Drag the arrow down a couple of lines (with the mouse button pressed), and the lines become selected.

**Clicking in the left margin selects the line.**

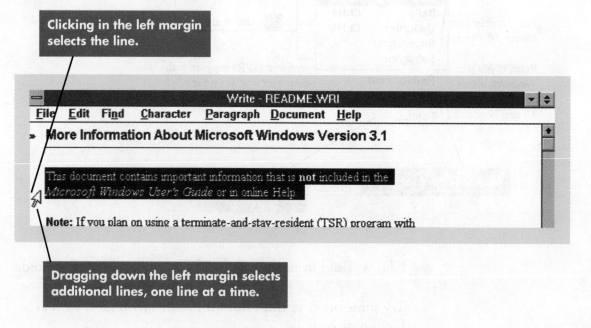

**Dragging down the left margin selects additional lines, one line at a time.**

**6.** Open the **Character** menu and choose **Fonts....**

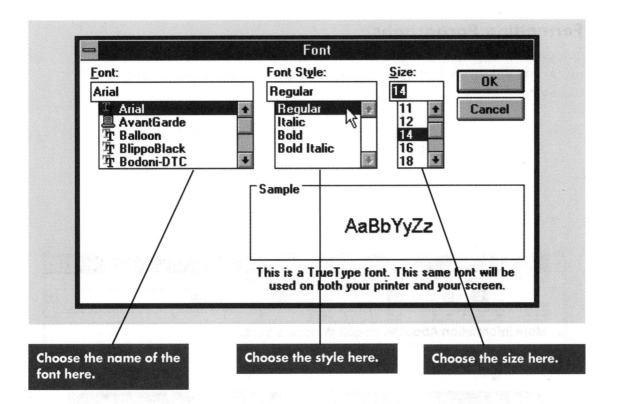

Choose the name of the font here.

Choose the style here.

Choose the size here.

Depending on what type of printer you have and the fonts installed in your system, you may or may not have the same fonts as in the picture above.

**7.** Choose any font you like, as well as its style and size. (You can see an example of the effect in the **Sample** section of the dialog box). **OK** the box, and the font will change.

**● Note** How do you change the font for *all* the text in an existing document? First, select all the text, by putting the arrow in the left margin, pressing **Ctrl** and clicking the mouse button. Then choose the font, as you did above.

## Formatting Paragraphs

You can do paragraph formatting with the Paragraph menu options
just as you did for character formatting, but there's a simpler way, using
the *Ruler*.

**1.** Open the **Document** menu and choose **Ruler On**. This
adds a bar at the top of the page, the Ruler, which contains
several buttons you can click on to quickly alter paragraph
formatting.

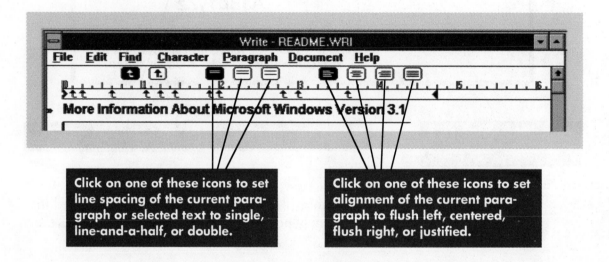

Click on one of these icons to set
line spacing of the current paragraph or selected text to single,
line-and-a-half, or double.

Click on one of these icons to set
alignment of the current paragraph to flush left, centered,
flush right, or justified.

Paragraph formatting is applied to the paragraph the cursor is in. You
don't have to actually select the text.

**2.** Move the cursor into the paragraph that starts with the
word *Note*.

**3.** Click on the **Right Alignment** button in the **Ruler**. (I've scrolled my text up a bit.)

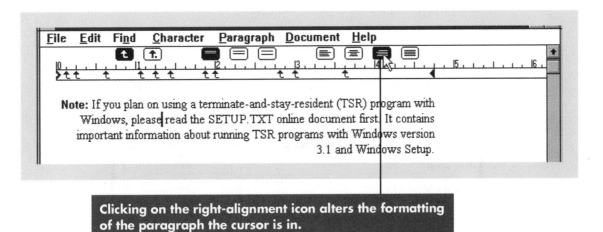

Clicking on the right-alignment icon alters the formatting of the paragraph the cursor is in.

**4.** Experiment with Centered and Justified alignment. Then check out the spacing options by clicking on them. It's neat how the text instantly reformats with just a click of the mouse, isn't it?

The other items on the ruler have to do with setting custom tabs. If you want to experiment with tabs, open the Write Help menu, choose Contents, and click on one of the Change Tabs topics for a complete discussion.

## Searching for Text

Write has a Search feature exactly like the one you experimented with in Cardfile and Notepad, except that it's called Find. With it, you can quickly locate words, even in huge documents. There's another notable feature on the Find menu, called Replace. Say you want to replace all occurrences of "DOS" with "MS-DOS." You'd do this:

**1.** Open the **Find** menu and choose **Replace**.

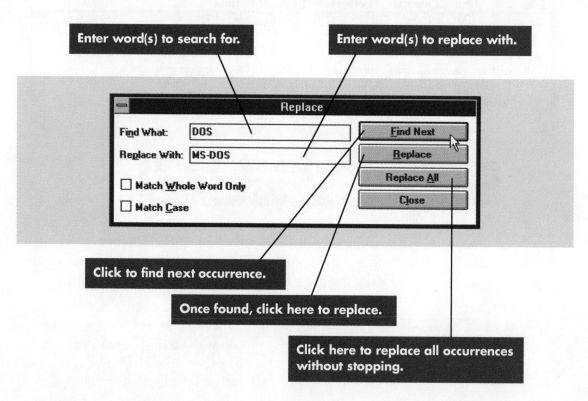

Enter word(s) to search for.

Enter word(s) to replace with.

Click to find next occurrence.

Once found, click here to replace.

Click here to replace all occurrences without stopping.

**2.** Type in the information as you see above.

**3.** Click on **Find Next**. The first occurrence of DOS is found, and becomes highlighted. Now you can click on **Replace** to change it, or move to the next occurrence of DOS by clicking on **Find Next**.

**● Note** Sometimes when using Find, or Replace, you won't be able to see the word that's been found, because it's hidden by the dialog box. You'll have to move the box (by dragging its title bar) to see the found word.

**4.** When you're finished using the Replace dialog box, click on **Close**.

## Undoing Your Mistakes

Murphy's law never takes a holiday when it comes to computers. Screwups happen all the time—like when the mouse slips too far and suddenly you've deleted that paragraph you just spent fifteen minutes perfecting.

Luckily the Undo command will reverse the last operation you perform, so it takes some of the anxiety out of experimenting with Write. Let's try one of the most common boo-boos as an example:

**1.** Select a paragraph. It doesn't matter which one.

**2.** Press the **Del** key. The paragraph disappears.

**3.** Panic momentarily (optional) until you remember the Undo command.

**4.** Open the **Edit** menu and choose **Undo Editing**. The paragraph miraculously reappears. Deselect it before you touch any keys or you might accidentally replace it by the next key press and have to use Undo again! If this were to happen, you could fix it by opening the Edit menu and choosing Undo *Typing*. (The command changes depending on what your last action was.) The easiest way to deselect any text is to single-click on it.

Remember that Undo can only undo your last action. This means that if, for example, you have used Replace and gone on to the *next* instance of the same word, only the last replacement will be undone. Incidentally, Undo can also be used to undo formatting changes.

That's it for Write. Now you know the basics. Printing is done just as you would imagine—from the File menu. Ditto for Saving. Now close the Readme document without saving the changes, since you may want to refer to its technical information later.

Between Notepad and Write you've got more than adequate word processing capability, and your skill is getting well-honed. All that's left to round out your working knowledge of Windows is learning how to create your own graphics using Paintbrush. So turn the page and let's finish up.

# 24

## Creating Graphic Art with Paintbrush

The last accessory program I'll cover in this book, Paintbrush, is similar to a number of other drawing programs on the market, such as PC Paintbrush, Mouse Paint, and PC Paint.

With Paintbrush you can create signs, technical drawings, illustrations, invitations, maps, and so on. Even if you aren't an artist, you'll have fun playing with Paintbrush.

## Starting a New Picture

Let's start drawing a new picture.

1. Open the **Accessories** group (as usual) and run **Paintbrush**. Maximize the Paintbrush window so it's as large as possible. (Remember the Maximize button in the upper-right corner of the window?)

*Quick & Easy*

Toolbox. Contains 18 different tools with which you can draw lines, curves, boxes, circles, and freehand shapes. Click on one to select it.

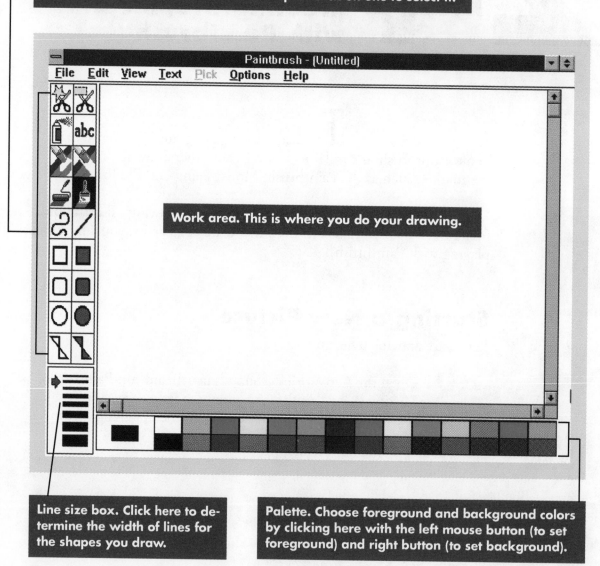

Paintbrush - [Untitled]

<u>F</u>ile   <u>E</u>dit   <u>V</u>iew   <u>T</u>ext   <u>P</u>ick   <u>O</u>ptions   <u>H</u>elp

Work area. This is where you do your drawing.

Line size box. Click here to determine the width of lines for the shapes you draw.

Palette. Choose foreground and background colors by clicking here with the left mouse button (to set foreground) and right button (to set background).

**2.** Move the mouse. Notice that a little dot moves around in the work area. This is because the **Brush** tool is selected in the toolbox to the left. Try pressing the mouse button and moving the mouse around. You'll draw a squiggly line!

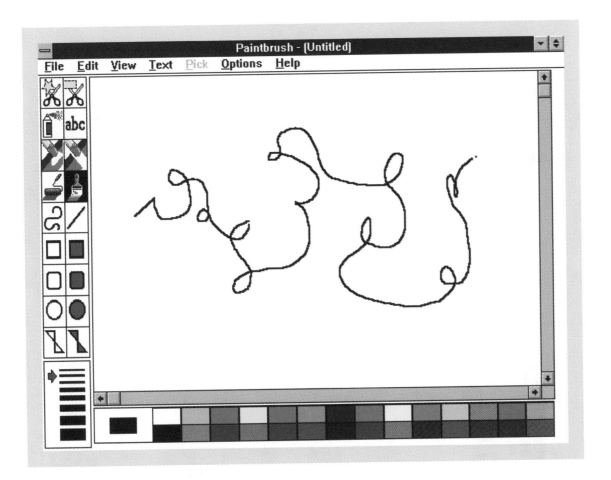

Not bad for your first try—anyway, you get the idea.

# Changing the Color

Now try changing the brush color before you draw the next line.

**1.** Click on one of the colors in the palette at the bottom of the screen.

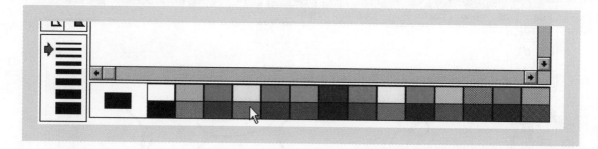

**2.** Now draw another line. It will be in the new color.

**3.** Now click on the **Line Size** palette in the lower-left side of the screen, to increase the line width, and draw another line. This one will be thicker.

● **Note**  Your lines don't all have to be continuous. You can draw short lines by releasing the mouse button to end a stroke, as you'd do with a paintbrush. Then reposition the brush and begin drawing again.

# Other Paintbrush Tools

OK. You've got the basics under control. What about all those other tools? Here's a little diagram of what each is called:

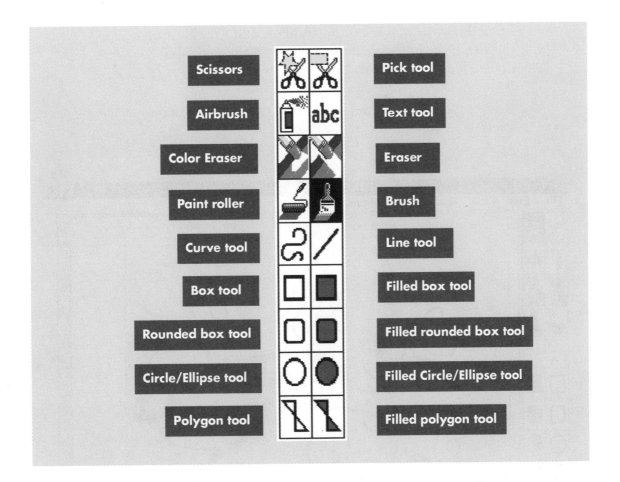

Let's try a couple of them, then you can experiment with the rest, since they're all pretty much the same. If you get stuck, use the Help system. Each tool is explained under the section called Tools (you have to scroll down one screenful on the Contents page to get to it).

**1.** First, if your screen is getting a little messy, let's clear some space to work in. Click on the upper-right scissors icon, the **Pick** tool.

**2.** Position the crosshair in the upper-left corner of the workspace. Press the mouse button and hold it down. Now drag the cursor across the screen diagonally to the right and down. This will outline a boxed area.

**3.** Release the mouse button. An area of the drawing is now selected, as you can see by the dashed line.

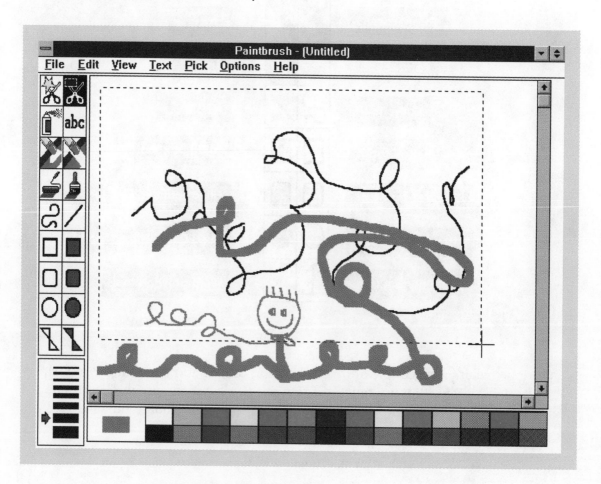

**4.** Open the **Edit** menu and choose **Cut**. Now the area is cleared. Incidentally, you use this Edit menu just as you did in other accessories. In fact you could now paste what you just cut into any program that will accept graphics—Write or Cardfile, for instance.

**5.** Click on the spray can icon, the **Airbrush** tool.

**6.** Choose a scintillating color from the palette, then one of the smallest line widths.

**7.** Start spray-painting graffiti on your canvas.

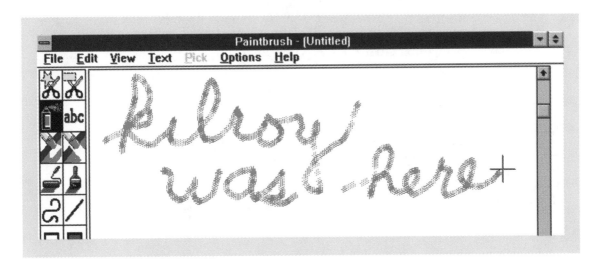

**8.** Click on the **Box** tool now. Position the cursor in the upper-left corner of the work area, and click and drag just as you did to select the area we cut out. When you release the mouse button, a box is drawn in the current color and line width.

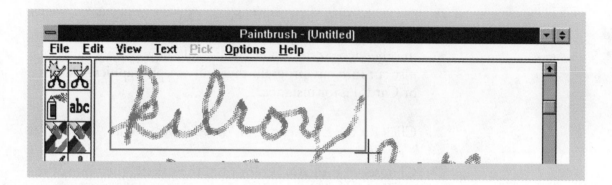

**9.** Finally, let's add text to the picture. This is fun because
you have access to any of the fonts installed in your system.
Click on the ABC icon, the **Text** tool. Choose a color. Now
position the cursor in some blank area and click. The cursor
changes to a text cursor. Now type something.

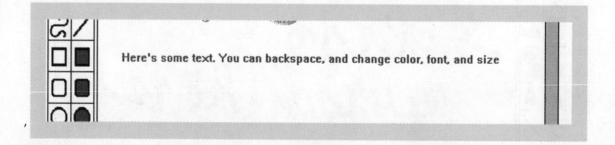

When you choose another tool, switch to a different application, or
use a scroll bar, what you've typed will be *pasted down*—it will become
permanent. But before that you can change the color by clicking on
the palette, or change the font with the Text menu. You can also correct
typing mistakes with **Backspace**. To remove text that's been pasted
down, select it with the Pick tool and cut it, or use the Eraser tool.

**● Note** Shapes you draw with the other tools also get pasted down. But before they are, you can undo them. Draw anything you want; then if you decide you don't like it open the Edit menu and choose Undo. If you want to remove text after it's been pasted down, it must be selected and then cut, or you can use the Erase tool. Before text has been pasted, **Backspace** will erase it.

**10.** Open the **Text** menu, choose **Font**, and change the font to *22 point Arial bold italic underline.* (On the way there, notice the special options on the Text menu. They work only with text.)

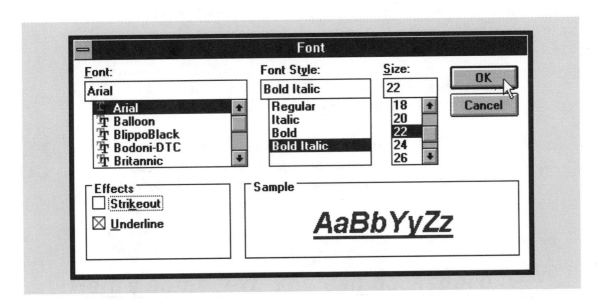

Now your text should look a bit like this:

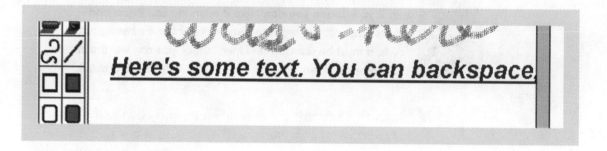

## Special Effects

Paintbrush has a few special effects that are fun to play with. Check them out on the Pick menu. I'll show you a couple (Flip and Inverse), and you can play with the others yourself.

**1.** Use the **Pick** tool (upper right-hand scissors) to draw a line around some of the the text you just enlarged.

**2.** Open the **Pick** menu and choose **Flip Horizontal**. Now you have a way of writing secret messages that can only be read in a mirror. (Flip Vertical turns your selection upside-down.)

**3.** Now select a large square somewhere in the middle of the screen.

**4.** Open the **Pick** menu and choose **Inverse**. Colors are inverted to their complements (those opposite them on the Red-Green-Blue color wheel).

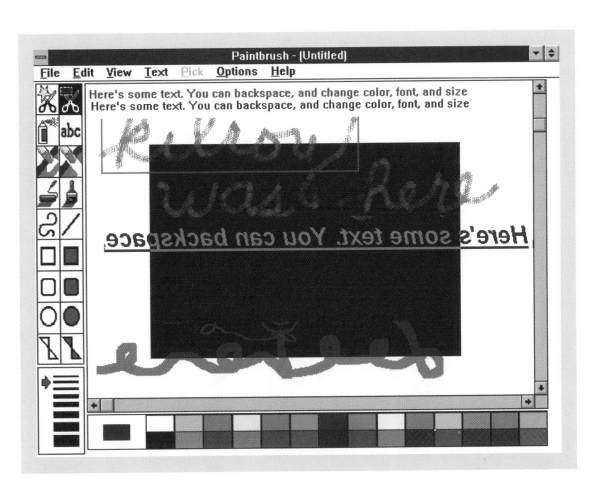

You've got the basics. Now let your imagination run wild. You can actually create some groovy and/or useful drawings with Paintbrush if you take the time and develop some dexterity with the mouse.

Well, that's about it for your introduction to Windows. I hope it's been survivable, and maybe even fun. The best advice now is just to start using Windows and Windows programs to get your everyday tasks done. Before you know it, you'll be an expert. Remember—when you're stuck, read the Help screens. And don't be afraid to experiment.

# Where Do
# I Go from Here?

Now you know the basics—everything you need to know to get up and running with Windows as quickly as possible. Eventually, though, you'll want to learn about all the powerful features available in Windows. For example, you may want to know how to configure your Windows setup by changing the screen colors, adding fonts to your applications, or customizing the way your mouse works. Or you might want to create complex documents that link several programs together using the Object Linking and Embedding (OLE) feature.

If you'd like to stick with a beginner's approach, learning in short, easy lessons and trying things out step-by-step, then *ABC's of Windows 3.1*, by Alan R. Neibauer (SYBEX, 1992) is the right book for you. It covers the material in this book with a little more explanation, and then continues on to explain some of the more useful advanced features.

If you think you're ready for a how-to book that covers Windows in-depth, try my other Windows book, *Mastering Windows 3.1 Special Edition* (SYBEX, 1992). It's full of great examples and hands-on steps, and it explains everything from the most basic topics to the most advanced. It also includes over 200 pages of troubleshooting information and timesaving tips and tricks that all Windows users will find extremely helpful.

# Help Yourself with
# Another Quality Sybex Book

## Windows 3.1
## Instant Reference
**Marshall L. Moseley**

Enjoy fast access to concise information on every Windows 3.1 mouse and keyboard command, including the accessory programs and Help facilities. Perfect for any Windows 3.1 user who needs an occasional on-the-job reminder.

262pp; 4 3/4" x 8"
**ISBN: 0-89588-844-0**

Available
at Better
Bookstores
Everywhere

Sybex Inc.
2021 Challenger Drive
Alameda, CA 94501
Telephone (800) 227-2346
Fax (510) 523-2373

# Sybex. Help Yourself.

# Help Yourself with
# Another Quality Sybex Book

## Mastering Windows 3.1
### Robert Cowart

The complete guide to installing, using, and making the most of Windows on IBM PCs and compatibles now in an up-to-date new edition. Part I provides detailed, hands-on coverage of major Windows features that are essential for day-to-day use. Part II offers complete tutorials on the accessory programs. Part III explores a selection of advanced topics.

600pp; 7 1/2" x 9"
**ISBN: 0-89588-842-4**

Available
at Better
Bookstores
Everywhere

Sybex Inc.
2021 Challenger Drive
Alameda, CA 94501
Telephone (800) 227-2346
Fax (510) 523-2373

# Sybex. Help Yourself.